Conten

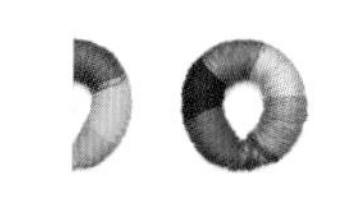

8

18

34

42

54

64

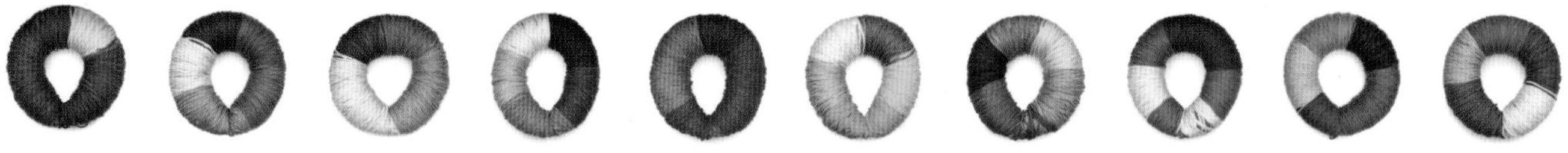
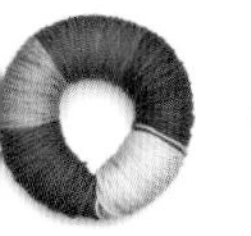
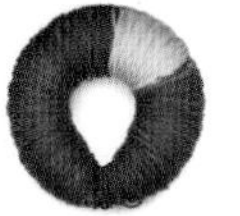
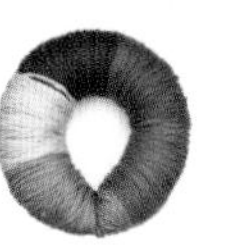
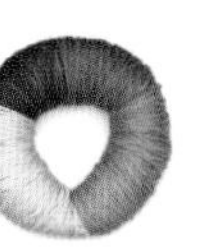
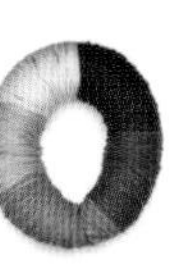
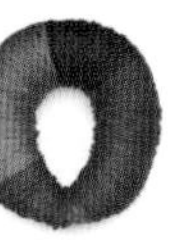

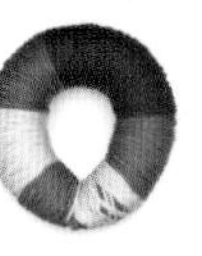
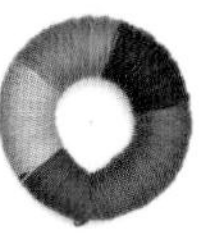
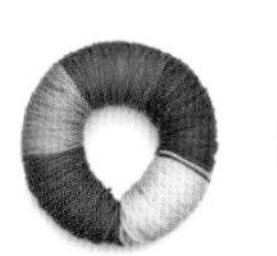

How to O'Go

O'Go is a whole new yarn format with smooth, tangle-free stitching and easy color changes. The colors in multicolored O'Gos are specially selected to create harmonious color arrangements, taking the mystery out of choosing colors.

GETTING STARTED

1. Snip

Gently locate the fastener cord where the two ends of the O'Go meet. Snip.

2. Pull

Holding the join, pull the fastener cord out of the O'Go.

3. Stitch

The yarn flows smoothly from the outside of the O'Go and will be tangle-free.

TWO WAYS TO O'GO

There are two ways to use your O'Go. For either method, you can use one or more O'Gos. Refer to the instructions for your project to see which method to use.

Caron® Colorama™ O'Go™ in Baja

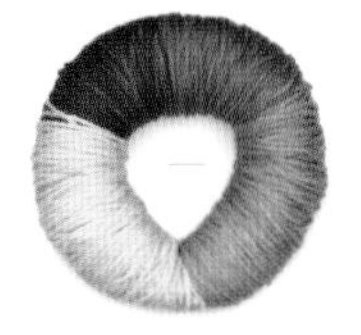
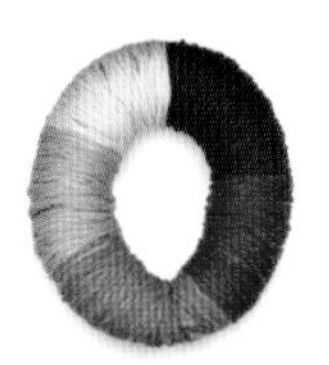
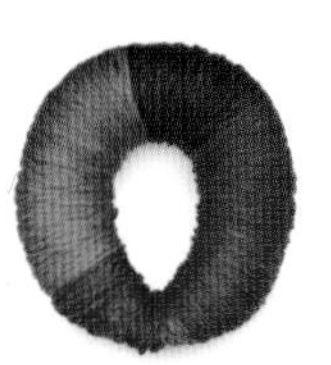
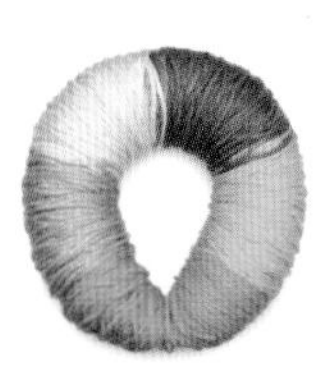

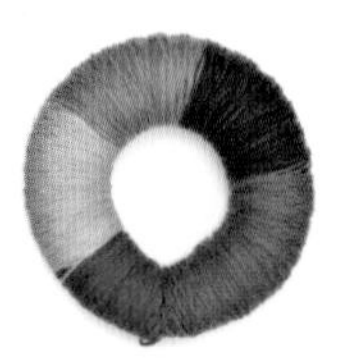

Break It. Make It.

Separate your colors to customize your color placement. To customize your colors, simply separate your O'Go into its color segments, then stitch them in any order you like, or follow the instructions for the project you're creating. Refer to the O'Go diagram in the materials section of your pattern to identify color A, B, C, etc. You may find it helpful to place each color section in its own resealable plastic bag and label the bag A, B, C, etc.

You can work with the yarn straight from the O'Go or separate the colors as shown.

Just O'Go

Instead of separating the colors, you can stitch through from one end to the other and let the stripes form themselves. Combining two or more different O'Gos will add even more fabulous color to your crochet projects.

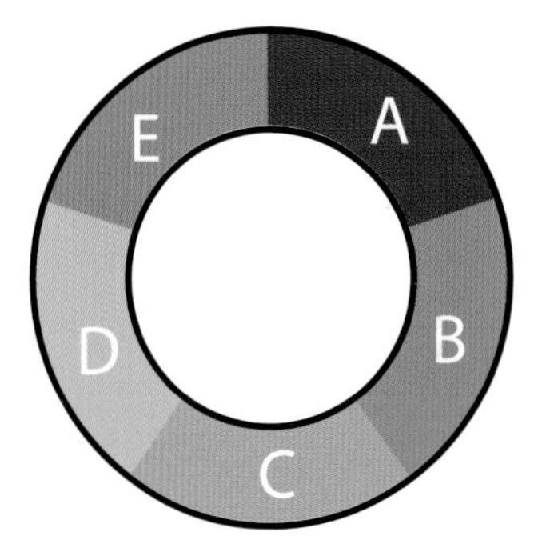

Follow the color guide for your chosen pattern to label each color within the O'Go.

Like all striping yarns, each O'Go is unique and might not start and end with the same color. If the shade you need isn't within reach, simply break it and make it using O'Go's easy color separation to get to the color you need. Then join your yarn and keep on stitching.

On the Go Knit Hat (page 46)

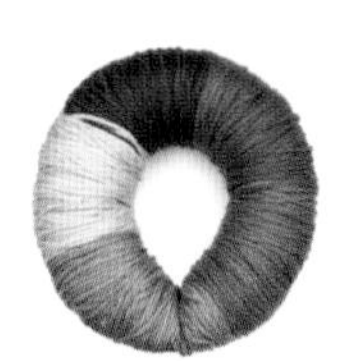
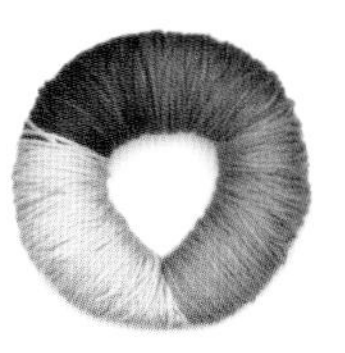
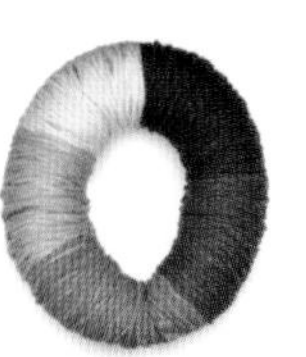

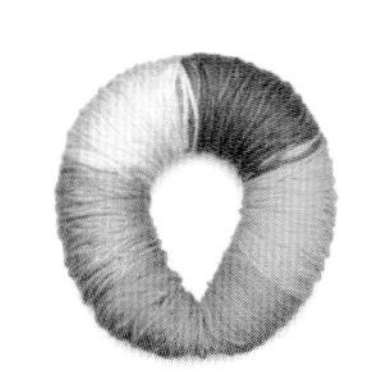

HIGHLIGHTER LINES HAT

Easy

SIZE

One size to fit average Adult.

MATERIALS

YARN

Red Heart® Super Saver™ O'Go™ Prints, 5oz/141g O'Gos, each approx 236yd/215m (acrylic) (4)

- 1 O'Go in #7124 Newsprint (A)

Red Heart® Super Saver™ O'Go™ Solids, 7oz/197g O'Gos, each approx 364yd/333m (acrylic) (4)

- 1 O'Go in #7160 Gold (B)

NEEDLES

- One pair size 7 (4.5mm) knitting needles, *or size needed to obtain gauge*
- One pair size 8 (5mm) knitting needles, *or size needed to obtain gauge*

NOTIONS

- Stitch marker
- Yarn needle

GAUGE

17 sts and 28 rows = 4"/10cm in pat with larger needles.
TAKE TIME TO CHECK GAUGE.

HAT

With B and smaller needles cast on 85 sts.

1st row: (RS). *K1. P1. Rep from * to last st. K1.

2nd row: *P1. K1. Rep from * to last st. P1.

Rep last 2 rows (K1. P1) ribbing for 3"/7.5cm, ending on a WS row. Place marker at end of last row.

Change to larger needles and proceed in pat as follows:

1st row: (RS). With A, K2. *Sl1Pwyib. K3. Rep from * to last 3 sts. Sl1Pwyib. K2.

2nd row: With A, K2. *Sl1Pwyif. K3. Rep from * to last 3 sts. Sl1Pwyif. K2.

3rd row: With A, K2. *With B, K1. With A, K3. Rep from * to last 3 sts. With B, K1. With A, K2.

4th row: As 2nd row.

5th row: As 1st row.

6th row: With A, K2. *With B, P1. With A, K3. Rep from * to last 3 sts. With B, P1. With A, K2.

Rep last 6 rows for pat until Hat from marked row measures approx 6"/15cm, ending on a 6th row of pat.

SHAPE TOP

1st row: (RS). With A, K2. *Sl1Pwyib. K1. K2tog. Rep from * to last 3 sts. Sl1Pwyib. K2. 65 sts.

2nd row: With A, K2. *Sl1Pwyif. K2. Rep from * to last 3 sts. Sl1Pwyif. K2.

3rd row: With A, K2. *With B, K1. With A, K2. Rep from * to last 3 sts. With B, K1. With A, K2.
4th row: As 2nd row.
5th row: With A, K2tog. *Sl1Pwyib. K2tog. Rep from * to last 3 sts. Sl1Pwyib. K2tog. 45 sts.
6th row: With A, K1. *With B, P1. With A, K1. Rep from * to last 2 sts. With B, P1. With A, K1.
7th row: With A, K1. *Sl1Pwyib. K1. Rep from * to last 2 sts. Sl1Pwyib. K1.
8th row: With A, K1. *Sl1Pwyif. K1. Rep from * to last 2 sts. Sl1Pwyif. K1. Break A.
9th row: With B, K1. *K2tog. Rep from * end of row. 23 sts.

FINISHING

Break yarn leaving a long end. Thread end onto yarn needle and draw tightly through rem sts. Sew center back seam, reversing seam for cuff turnback.

POMPOM

Wind B around 4 fingers 100 times. Tie tightly in the middle and leave a long end for attaching to Hat. Cut loops at both ends and trim to smooth round shape. Sew securely to top of Hat. •

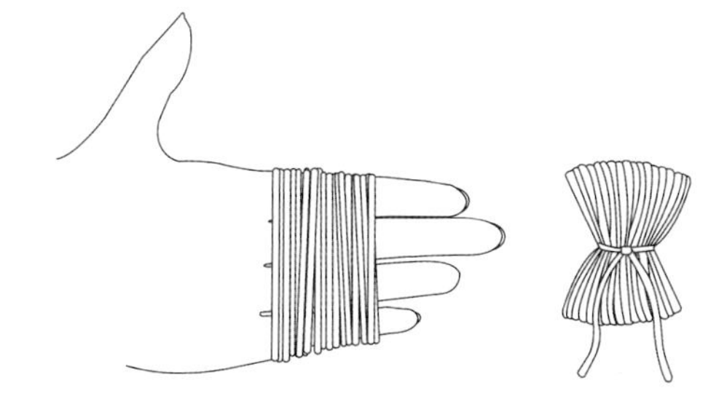

BEGINNER BIAS STRIPED BLANKET

Basic

MEASUREMENTS

Approx 48"/123cm wide x 50"/127cm long.

MATERIALS

YARN

Bernat® Blanket™ O'Go™, 10.5oz/300g O'Gos, each approx 220yd/201m (polyester)

- 2 O'Gos in #42019 Rose Gold (A)
- 2 O'Gos in #42004 Toasted Almond (B)

NEEDLE

- One size 11 (8mm) circular needle, 29"/73.5cm long, *or size needed to obtain gauge.*

NOTION

- Yarn needle

GAUGE

7 sts and 14 rows = 4"/10cm in garter st.

TAKE TIME TO CHECK GAUGE.

NOTE

Do not break yarn when changing colors, carry color not in use loosely up side of work.

STRIPE PAT

With A, work 2 rows.

With B, work 2 rows.

These 4 rows form Stripe Pat.

BLANKET

With A, cast on 2 stitches (sts).

1st row: (Kfb) twice. 4 sts.

2nd row: K2. Yo. Knit to end of row. Join B.

3rd and 4th rows: With B, as 2nd row. Join A at end of last row.

5th and 6th rows: With A, as 2nd row. Join B at end of last row.

Stripe Pat is now in position.

Keeping continuity (cont) of Stripe Pat, rep 2nd row until work measures approx 48"/123cm along straight side edge, ending with 2 rows of B.

Keeping cont of Stripe Pat, proceed as follows:

1st row: (RS). With A, K1. K2tog. yo. K2tog. Knit to end of row.

2nd row: K2. yo. Knit to end of row.

Keeping cont of Stripe Pat, rep last 2 rows 5 times more.

Next row: (WS). K1. K2tog. yo. K2tog. Knit to end of row.

Keeping cont of Stripe Pat, rep last row until there are 2 sts.

Next row: K2tog. Fasten off by cutting yarn and drawing tightly through last st. •

GOTTA SPLIT BRIOCHE COWL

Basic

MEASUREMENTS

Approx 24"/61cm tall x 32"/81cm in diameter at bottom and 22½"/57cm in diameter at top.

MATERIALS

YARN

Caron® Colorama™ O'Go™, 6.4oz/180g O'Gos, each approx 228yd/208m (acrylic) (5)

- 1 O'Go in #68021 Biker Jacket (A)
- 1 O'Go in #68009 First Blush (B)

NEEDLES

- One size 9 (5.5mm) circular needle, 16"/41cm long, *or size needed to obtain gauge.*
- One size 9 (5.5mm) circular needle, 29"/73.5cm long, *or size needed to obtain gauge.*

Optional: One size 10½ (6.5mm) circular needle, 29"/73.5cm long for looser cast on.

NOTIONS

- Stitch marker
- Yarn needle

GAUGE

10 sts and 28 rows = 4"/10cm with smaller needles in Brioche stitch. *TAKE TIME TO CHECK GAUGE.*

STITCH GLOSSARY

See inside back cover for instructions for brioche techniques.

NOTES

1) The wrap (yarn over) created by Sl1yo does not count as a separate stitch and should be treated as 1 stitch along with slipped stitch it accompanies.

2) Work is turned every second row.

3) Optional: Use larger needle for ease of working loose cast on and bind off.

COWL

With longer circular needle and A, cast on 81 sts loosely (optional: use larger needle). Do not join. Working back and forth across needle in rows, proceed as follows:

1st row: (RS). With A, K1. (Sl1yo. K1) 3 times. *Sl1yo. P1. Rep from * to last 8 sts. (Sl1yo. K1) 4 times. Do not turn. Slide sts to opposite end of needle.

2nd row: (RS). With B, Sl1Pwyif. (BrP1. Sl1yo) 3 times *BrK1. Sl1yo. Rep from * to last 8 sts. BrK1. (Sl1yo. BrP1) 3 times Sl1Pwyif. Turn.

3rd row: (WS). With A, P1. (Sl1yo. BrP1) 3 times. *Sl1yo. BrK1. Rep from * to last 8 sts. Sl1yo. (BrP1. Sl1yo) 3 times. P1. Do not turn. Slide sts to opposite end of needle.

4th row: (WS). With B, Sl1Pwyib. (BrK1. Sl1yo) 3 times. *BrP1. Sl1yo. Rep from * to last 7 sts. Sl1yo (BrK1. Sl1yo) 3 times. Sl1Pwyib. Turn.

5th row: (RS). With A, K1. (Sl1yo. BrK1) 3 times. *Sl1yo. BrP1. Rep from * to last 8 sts. (Sl1yo. BrK1) 3 times. Sl1yo. K1. Do not turn. Slide sts to opposite end of needle.

6th row: (RS). With B, Sl1Pwyif. (BrP1. Sl1yo) 3 times *BrK1. Sl1yo. Rep from * to last 8 sts. BrK1. (Sl1yo. BrP1) 3 times. Sl1Pwyif. Turn.

Rep 3rd to 6th rows until work from beg measures approx 8"/20.5cm ,ending on a 6th row and ending last rep with Sl1Pwyib. Do not turn at the end of last row.

With RS facing, beg working in rnds as follows:

1st rnd: Sl last st of prev row to left-hand needle. PM for beg of rnd. With A, K2tog. (Sl1yo. BrK1) 3 times. *Sl1yo. BrP1. Rep from * to last 7 sts. (Sl1yo. BrK1) 3 times. Sl1yo. 80 sts.

GOTTA SPLIT BRIOCHE COWL

2nd rnd: With B, (Sl1yo. BrP1) 3 times. *Sl1yo. BrK1. Rep from * to last 6 sts. (Sl1yo. BrP1) 3 times.
3rd rnd: With A, (Brk1. Sl1yo) 4 times. *BrP1. Sl1yo. Rep from * to last 6 sts. (BrK1. Sl1yo) 3 times.
Rep last 2 rnds for pat until work from joining in rnd measures approx 4"/10cm, ending on a 3rd rnd.

Dec as follows:
Next rnd: With B, (Sl1yo. BrP1) 3 times. Sl1yo. BrDecL. (Sl1yo. BrK1) 10 times. Sl1yo. BrDecR. (Sl1yo. BrK1) 6 times. Sl1yo. BrDecL. (Sl1yo. BrK1) 10 times. Sl1yo. BrDecR. (Sl1yo. BrP1) 3 times. 72 sts.
Beg with A rnd, work 27 rnds even in pat.

Change to shorter circular needle.
Next rnd: With B, (Sl1yo. BrP1) 3 times. Sl1yo. BrDecL. (Sl1yo. BrK1) 8 times. Sl1yo. BrDecR. (Sl1yo. BrK1) 6 times. Sl1yo. BrDecL. (Sl1yo. BrK1) 8 times. Sl1yo. BrDecR. (Sl1yo. BrP1) 3 times. 64 sts.
Beg with A rnd, work 27 rnds even in pat.

Next rnd: With B, (Sl1yo. BrP1) 3 times. Sl1yo. BrDecL. (Sl1yo. BrK1) 6 times. Sl1yo. BrDecR. (Sl1yo. BrK1) 6 times. Sl1yo. BrDecL. (Sl1yo. BrK1) 6 times. Sl1yo. BrDecR. (Sl1yo. BrP1) 3 times. 56 sts.
Beg with A rnd, work 27 rnds even in pat.
Break B.

Next rnd: With A, (K1. BrkP1) 3 times. K1. *BrK1. P1. Rep from * to last 7 sts. BrK1. (K1. BrkP1) 3 times.
Cast off loosely in ribbing (optional: use larger needle). •

CITY WALKS SWEATER VEST

Basic

SIZES

To fit bust measurement:

XS/S 28–34"/71–86.5cm

M 36–38"/91.5–96.5cm

L 40–42"/101.5–106.5cm

XL 44–46"/112–117cm

2/3XL 48–54"/122–137cm

4/5XL 56–62"/142–157.5cm

Finished bust:

XS/S 39½"/108cm

M 45½"/117cm

L 49"/127cm

XL 51½"/136cm

2/3XL 55½"/155cm

4/5XL 61½"/157.5cm

MATERIALS

YARN

Caron® Colorama™ O'Go™, 6.4oz/180g O'Gos, each approx 228yd/208m (acrylic) (5)

- 2 (3, 3, 3, 4, 4) O'Gos in #68009 First Blush
- 2 (3, 3, 3, 4, 4) O'Gos in #68015 Blue Mustang

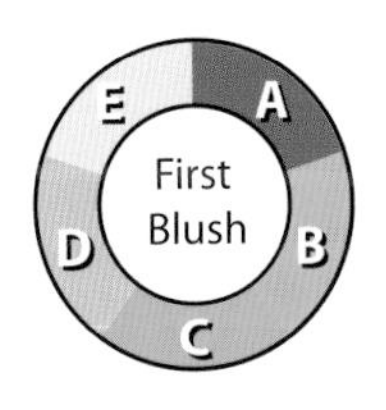

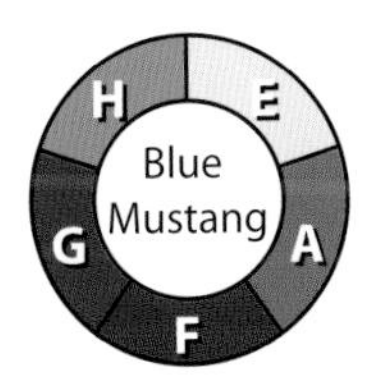

NEEDLES

- One pair size 8 (5mm) knitting needles, *or size needed to obtain gauge*
- One pair size 10 (6mm) knitting needles, *or size needed to obtain gauge*
- One size 8 (5mm) circular needle, 24"/51cm long, *or size needed to obtain gauge.*

NOTIONS

- Stitch markers
- Stitch holder
- Yarn needle

GAUGE

13 sts and 18 rows = 4"/10cm in St st with larger needles.

TAKE TIME TO CHECK GAUGE.

STITCH GLOSSARY

P2sso Pass 2 slipped stitches together over last st.

Sl2K Slip next 2 stitches knitwise together.

STRIPE PAT

With A, 16 rows.

*With F, 8 rows.

With G, 8 rows.

CITY WALKS SWEATER VEST

With E, 4 rows.
With H, 8 rows.
With E, 4 rows.
With B, 8 rows.
With E, 4 rows.
With D, 8 rows.
With E, 4 rows.
With C, 8 rows.
With E, 4 rows.
With H, 8 rows.
With E, 4 rows.
With G, 8 rows.
With F, 8 rows.
With E, 4 rows.
These 116 rows form Stripe Pat.
Rep Stripe Pat from * as needed to complete Vest.

NOTES

1) For this pattern, the colors in the O'Go need to be separated (see page 2 for tips).
2) Vest is worked flat in 2 pieces from bottom-up. Front and Back are seamed and sts picked up around armhole and neck for ribbed bands are worked in the round.
3) The instructions are written for smallest size. If changes are necessary for larger sizes the instructions will be written thus ( ). When only one number is given, it applies to all sizes.

FRONT

**Beg at lower edge, with A and smaller needles, cast on 63 (73-81-85-91-101) sts.
1st row: (RS). K1. *P1. K1. Rep from * to end of row.
2nd row: P1. *K1. P1. Rep from * to end of row.
First 2 rows of Stripe Pat are complete.
Keeping cont of Stripe Pat, rep last 2 rows of (K1. P1) ribbing for 3"/7.5cm, inc 3 (3-1-1-1-1) st(s) evenly across last row and ending on WS row. 66 (76-82-86-92-102) sts.

Change to larger needles and keeping cont of Stripe Pat, proceed as follows:
1st row: (RS). Knit.
2nd row: Purl.
3rd row: K1. *K1. P1. Rep from * to last st. K1.
4th row: Purl.
These 4 rows form Texture Pat.

Keeping cont of Stripe Pat, rep last 4 rows for Texture Pat until work from beg measures 11 (12-12-12-12-12)"/28 (30.5-30.5-30.5-30.5-30.5)cm, ending on a WS row.

SHAPE ARMHOLES

Keeping cont of pat, cast off 1 (3-5-6-9-10) st(s) at beg of next 2 rows. 64 (70-72-74-74-82) sts.**

SHAPE ARMHOLE AND LEFT FRONT NECK

1st row: (RS). K1 (armhole edge). ssk. Pat across 26 (29-30-31-31-35) sts. K2tog. K1 (neck edge). Turn. Leave rem sts on a spare needle.

Cont across 30 (33-34-35-35-39) sts as follows:
2nd row: Work even in pat.
3rd row: K1. ssk. Pat to last 3 sts. K2tog. K1. 28 (31-32-33-33-37) sts.
Rep last 2 rows 2 (3-3-3-2-3) time(s) more, then 2nd row once. 24 (25-26-27-29-31) sts.

SIZE 4/5XL ONLY

Next row: (RS). K1. ssk. Pat to last 3 sts. K2tog. K1. 29 sts.
Next row: Work even in pat.
Next row: K1. ssk. Pat to end of row. 28 sts.
Next row: Work even in pat.

ALL SIZES:

Dec 1 st at neck edge only on next and every following 4th row until 12 (13-14-14-15-15) sts rem, ending on a WS row.

CITY WALKS SWEATER VEST

SHAPE SHOULDER

1st row: (RS). Cast off 3 (4-2-2-3-3) sts. Pat to end of row. 9 (9-12-12-12-12) sts.

2nd row: Pat to last st. Sl1Pwyif. Turn.

3rd row: (Sl1Pwyib) twice. Pass first st over 2nd st – 1 st bound off. Cast off 2 (2-3-3-3-3) more sts. Pat to end of row. 6 (6-8-8-8-8) sts.

Rep last 2 rows twice more.

With RS facing, join yarn to rem sts.

SHAPE ARMHOLE AND RIGHT FRONT NECK

1st row: (RS). K1 (neck edge). ssk. Pat to last 3 sts. K2tog. K1 (armhole edge). 30 (33-34-35-35-39) sts rem.

2nd row: Work even in pat.

3rd row: K1. ssk. Pat to last 3 sts. K2tog. K1. 28 (31-32-33-33-37) sts.

Rep last 2 rows 2 (3-3-3-2-3) time(s) more, then 2nd row once. 24 (25-26-27-29-31) sts.

SIZE 4/5XL ONLY:

Next row: (RS). K1. ssk. Pat to last 3 sts. K2tog. K1. 29 sts.

Next row: Work even in pat.

Next row: Pat to last 3 sts. K2tog. K1. 28 sts.

Next row: Work even in pat.

ALL SIZES:

Dec 1 st at neck edge only on next and every following 4th row until 12 (13-14-14-15-15) sts rem, ending on a RS row.

SHAPE SHOULDER

1st row: (WS). Cast off 3 (4-2-2-3-3) sts. Pat to end of row. 9 (9-12-12-12-12) sts.

2nd row: Pat to last st. Sl1Pwyib. Turn.

3rd row: (Sl1Pwyif) twice. Pass first st over 2nd st – 1 st bound off. Cast off 2 (2-3-3-3-3) more sts. Pat to end of row. 6 (6-8-8-8-8) sts.

Rep last 2 rows twice more.

BACK

Work from ** to ** as given for Front.

Next row: (RS). K1. ssk. Pat to last 3 sts. K2tog. K1.

Next row: Work even in pat.

Rep last 2 rows 3 (4-4-4-3-6) times more. 56 (60-62-64-66-68) sts.

Cont even in pat until armhole measures same length as Front, ending on a WS row.

SHAPE SHOULDERS

1st row: (RS). Cast off 3 (4-2-2-3-3) sts. Pat to end of row. 53 (56-62-62-63-65) sts.

2nd row: Cast off 3 (4-2-2-3-3) sts. Pat to last st. Sl1Pwyif. 50 (52-60-60-60-62) sts.

3rd row: (Sl1Pwyib) twice. Pass first st over 2nd st – 1 st bound off. Cast off 2 (2-3-3-3-3) sts more. Pat to last st. Sl1Pwyib. 47 (49-56-56-56-58) sts.

4th row: (Sl1Pwyif) twice. Pass first st over 2nd st – 1 st bound off. Cast off 2 (2-3-3-3-3) sts more. Pat to last st. Sl1Pwyif. 44 (46-52-52-52-54) sts.

Rep last 2 rows twice more.

Leave rem 32 (34-36-36-36-38) sts on back neck st holder.

FINISHING

Pin to measurements on a flat surface. Cover with a damp cloth, leaving cloth to dry.

Sew shoulder seams as shown in diagram.

Taking care to align stripes, sew Front and Back side seams using mattress st, as shown in diagram, starting at top of Ribbing (leaving Ribbing open for split-hem).

ARMBANDS

With RS facing, A and circular needle, beg at side seam, pick up and knit 1 (3-5-6-9-10) st(s) across cast off sts. Pick up and knit 41 (42-42-45-47-48) sts up armhole to shoulder seam. Pick up and knit 41 (42-42-45-47-48) sts down armhole to cast off sts. Pick up and knit 1 (3-5-6-9-10) st(s) across rem cast off sts. 84 (90-94-102-112-116) sts. Join in rnd. PM for beg of rnd.

Next rnd: *K1. P1. Rep from * around.

Rep last rnd (K1. P1) ribbing for 1½"/4cm.

Cast off in ribbing.

NECKBAND

With RS facing, A and circular needle, K32 (34-36-36-36-38) sts from back neck st holder. Pick up and knit 48 (50-50-54-56-56) sts down left front neck edge. Pick up and knit 1 st between 2 sts at base of V-neck. PM on last st for center st. Pick up and knit 48 (50-50-54-56-56) sts up right front neck edge. Join in rnd. PM for beg of rnd. 129 (135-137-145-149-151) sts.

1st rnd: P1. *K1. P1. Rep from * to 1 st before center st marker. Sl2K. K1. P2sso. PM on last st for center st. **P1. K1. Rep from ** to last st. P2tog over last st and first st of next rnd. 126 (132-134-142-146-148) sts. Join in rnd. PM for beg of rnd.

2nd rnd: Work in (K1. P1) ribbing as established.

3rd rnd: Rib to 1 st before center marked st. Sl2K. K1. P2sso. PM on last st. Rib to end of rnd. 124 (130-132-140-144-146) sts.

Rep last 2 rnds twice more. 120 (126-128-136-140-142) sts.

Cast off in ribbing. •

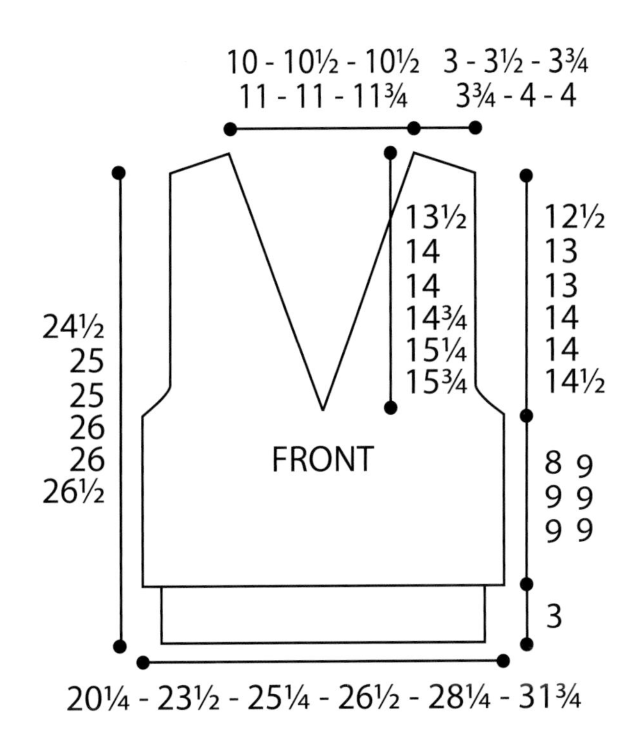

MATTRESS STITCH

SHOULDER SEAM

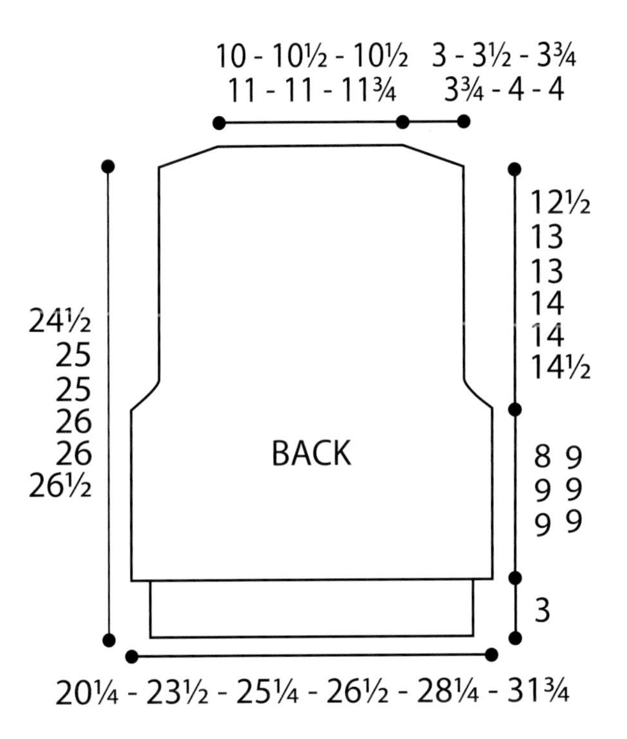

GO AROUND FAIR ISLE HAT

Basic

SIZE:

One size to fit Adult.

MATERIALS

YARN

Caron® Colorama™ O'Go™, 6.4oz/180g O'Gos, each approx 228yd/208m (acrylic) (5)

- 1 O'Go in #68016 Overboard

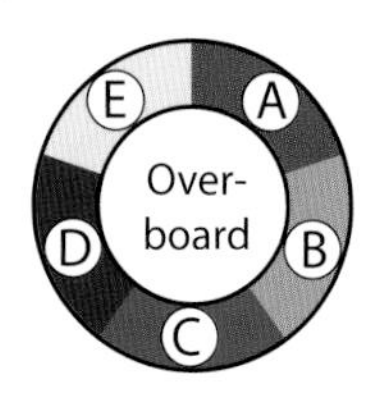

NEEDLES

- One set (4) double-pointed needles (dpn) size 9 (5.5mm), *or size needed to obtain gauge*
- One set (4) double-pointed needles (dpn) size 10 (6mm), *or size needed to obtain gauge*

NOTIONS

- Stitch marker
- Yarn needle

GAUGE

13 sts and 18 rows = 4"/10cm with larger needles in St st. *TAKE TIME TO CHECK GAUGE.*

STITCH GLOSSARY

Center Dec (worked over 3 sts) Slip next 2 stitches as if to K2tog. K1, then pass slipped sts over knit st—center of 3 sts should be on top of decrease, 2 sts have been decreased.

NOTES

1) For this pattern, the colors in the O'Go need to be separated (see page 2 for tips).

2) When working from charts, carry yarn not in use loosely across WS of work but never over more than 5 sts. When it must pass over more than 5 sts, weave it over and under color not in use. The colors are never twisted around one another.

HAT

With A and set of smaller double-pointed needles, cast on 64 sts. Divide sts over 3 needles (20-20-24). Join in rnd, placing marker on first st.

1st to 8th rnds: *K2. P2. Rep from * around. Break A.

Change to E and larger set of needles.
With E, knit 4 rnds.
Knit rnds 1 to 16 of Chart, reading rows from right to left, noting 4-st rep will be worked 16 times. Break C and E.

With B, shape top as follows:

1st rnd: *K7. Center Dec. K6. Rep from * around. 56 sts.
2nd and alt rnds: Knit.
3rd rnd: *K6. Center Dec. K5. Rep from * around. 48 sts.
5th rnd: *K5. Center Dec. K4. Rep from * around. 40 sts.
7th rnd: *K4. Center Dec. K3. Rep from * around. 32 sts.

9th rnd: *K3. Center Dec. K2. Rep from * around. 24 sts.

10th rnd: *K2tog. Rep from * around. 12 sts.

Break yarn, leaving a long end. Thread end through rem sts and draw up tightly. Fasten securely

FINISHING

POMPOM

Wind D around 4 fingers approx 80 times. Remove from fingers and tie tightly in center. Cut through each side of loops. Trim to a smooth round shape. Sew to top of Hat. •

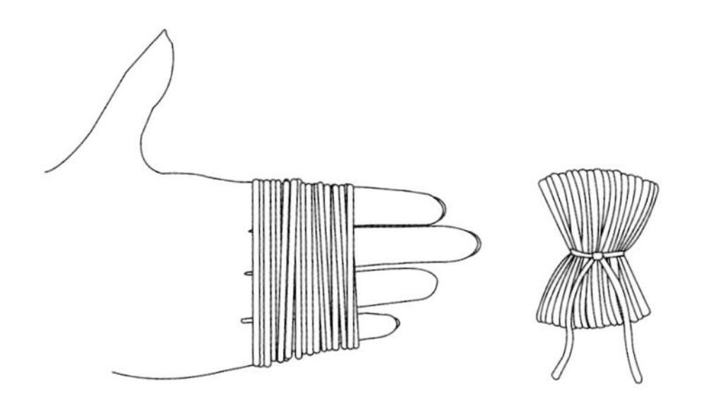

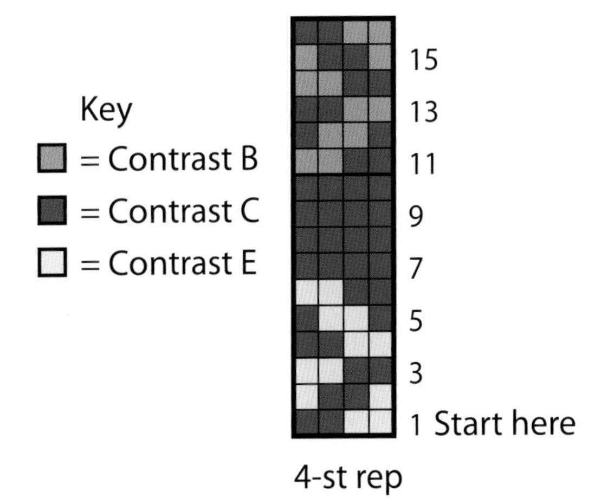

PIANO KEYS MITTENS

Intermediate

SIZE

One size to fit Adult.

MATERIALS

YARN

Caron® Big Donut™ O'Go™, 9.9oz/280g O'Gos, each approx 502yd/459m (acrylic) (4)

- 1 O'Go in #29002 Lemon Plum or #29005 Blue Moon

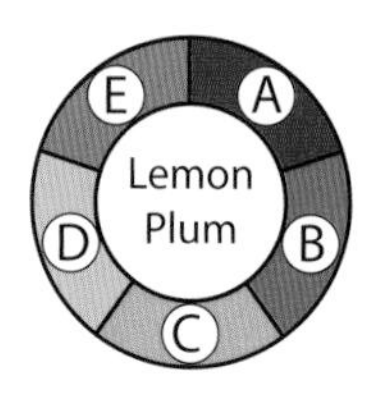

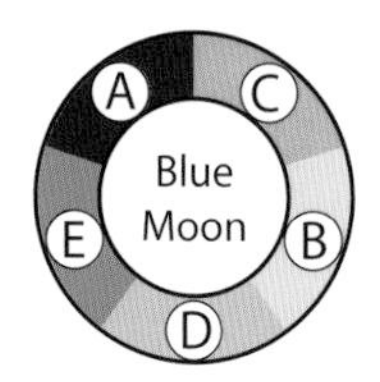

NEEDLES

- One set (4) double-pointed needles (dpn) size 6 (4mm), *or size needed to obtain gauge*
- One set (4) double-pointed needles (dpn) size 7 (4.5mm), *or size needed to obtain gauge*

NOTIONS

- Yarn needle
- Stitch marker

GAUGE

20 sts and 25 rows = 4"/10cm in Fair Isle Pat with larger needles. *TAKE TIME TO CHECK GAUGE.*

NOTES

1) For this pattern, the colors in the O'Go need to be separated (see page 2 for tips).

2) When working from chart, carry yarn not in use loosely across WS of work. The colors are never twisted around one another.

PIANO KEYS MITTENS

RIGHT MITTEN

**With set of 4 smaller needles and E, cast on 40 sts. Divide onto 3 needles (12, 12, 16) sts. PM on first st for beg of rnd.
1st rnd: *K2. P2. Rep from * around.
Rep last rnd of (K2. P2) ribbing for 2½"/6cm.**

Knit 1st to 16th rnds of Right Mitten Chart I, reading rnds from right to left.

Thumb Opening

1st rnd: Pat across 28 sts. Slip last 8 sts onto a st holder. Pat to end of rnd.
2nd rnd: Pat 20 sts. Turn. Cast on 8 sts. Turn. Pat to end of rnd. 40 sts.

***Cont in chart, noting 4-st decs on every rnd after 35th rnd.
Graft 2 sets of 2 sts tog (see diagrams at right).

Make Thumb

With E and larger needles, K8 from st holder. Pick up and knit 8 sts at base of thumb. Divide these 16 sts onto 3 needles (5, 5, 6). Join in rnd. PM on first st.
Next rnd: (K3. K2tog) 3 times. K1. 13 sts.
Knit 14 rnds even.
Next rnd: (K2tog) 6 times. K1. 7 sts. Break yarn. Thread end through rem 7 sts and fasten securely.***

LEFT MITTEN

Work from ** to ** as given for Right Mitten.

Knit 1st to 16th rnds of Left Mitten Chart II, reading rnds from right to left.

Thumb Opening

1st rnd: Pat across 20 sts. Slip last 8 sts onto a st holder. Pat to end of rnd.
2nd rnd: Pat 12 sts. Turn. Cast on 8 sts. Turn. Pat to end of rnd. 40 sts.

Work from *** to *** as given for Right Mitten. •

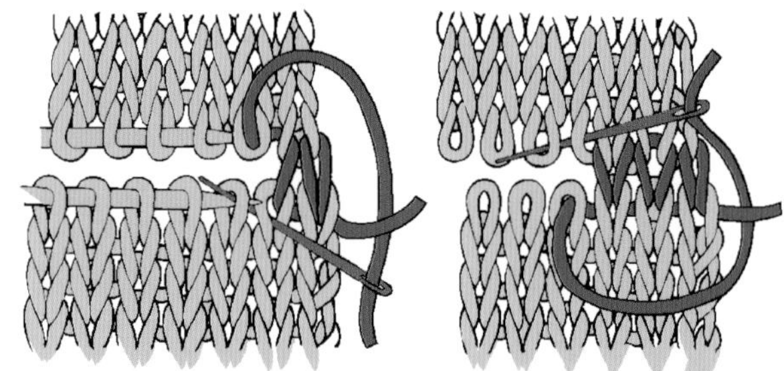

GRAFTING

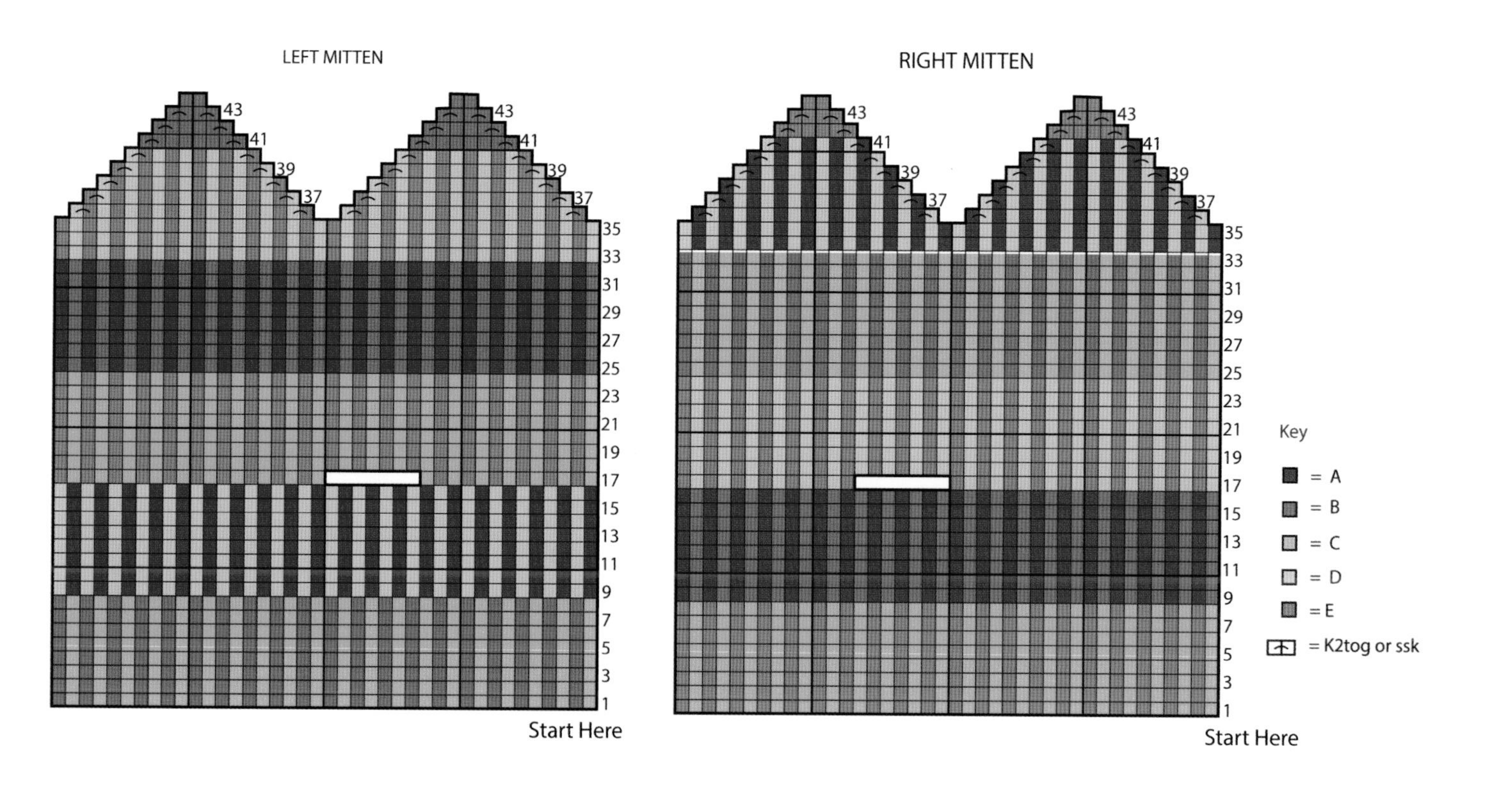
LEFT MITTEN
43
41
39
37
35
33
31
29
27
25
23
21
19
17
15
13
11
9
7
5
3
1
Start Here
RIGHT MITTEN
43
41
39
37
35
33
31
29
27
25
23
21
19
17
15
13
11
9
7
5
3
1
Start Here
Key
= A
= B
= C
= D
= E
= K2tog or ssk

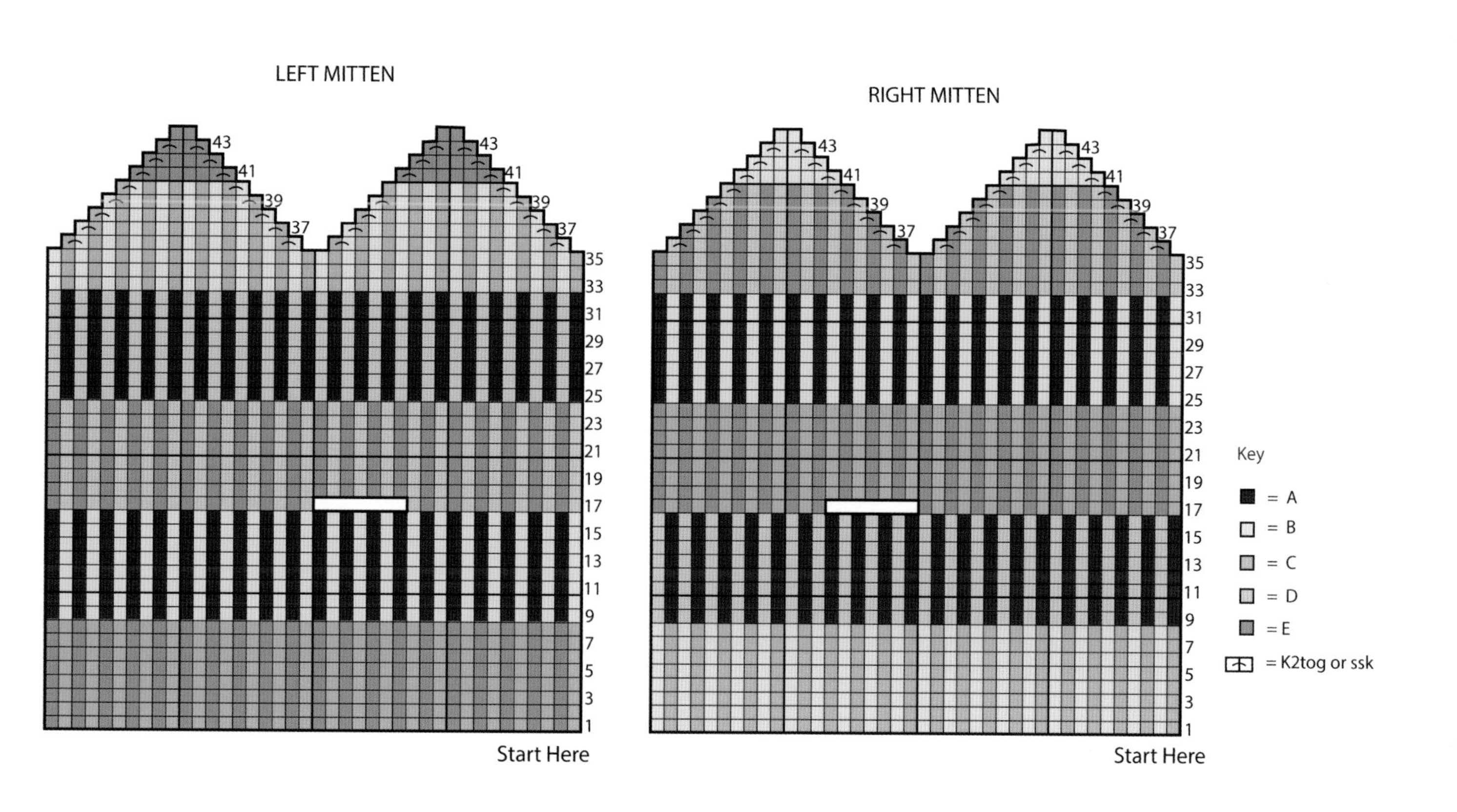
LEFT MITTEN
43
41
39
37
35
33
31
29
27
25
23
21
19
17
15
13
11
9
7
5
3
1
Start Here
RIGHT MITTEN
43
41
39
37
35
33
31
29
27
25
23
21
19
17
15
13
11
9
7
5
3
1
Start Here
Key
= A
= B
= C
= D
= E
= K2tog or ssk

BRIOCHE CABLES HAT

Basic

SIZE
One size to fit average Adult.

MATERIALS
YARN
Caron® Colorama™ O'Go™, 6.4oz/180g O'Gos, each approx 228yd/208m (acrylic) (5)

- 1 O'Go in #68009 First Blush (A, B, C, D, E)
- 1 O'Go in #68004 Lippy (D, E, F, G, H)

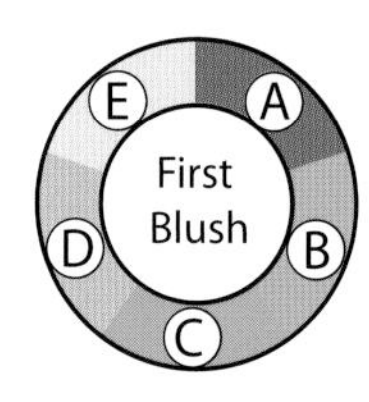

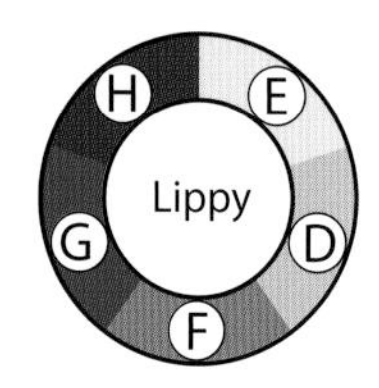

NEEDLES
- One size 8 (5mm) circular needle, 16"/40.5cm long, *or size needed to obtain gauge.*
- One size 10 (6mm) circular needle, 16"/40.5cm long, *or size needed to obtain gauge.*
- One set (4) double-pointed needles (dpn) size 8 (5mm), *or size needed to obtain gauge*

NOTIONS
- Stitch marker
- Yarn needle

GAUGE
12 sts and 32 rows = 4"/10cm in brioche pat on smaller needles.

13 sts and 20 rows = 4"/10cm in twisted rib pat on larger needles. *TAKE TIME TO CHECK GAUGE.*

STITCH GLOSSARY
See inside back cover for instructions for brioche techniques.

STRIPE PAT
Note: Stripe Pat refers to odd-numbered rnds only. All even-numbered rnds are worked in E.

With B, work 5 rnds.
With F, work 5 rnds.
With C, work 5 rnds.
With G, work 5 rnds.
With D, work 5 rnds.
With H, work 5 rnds.
These 30 rnds form Stripe Pat for odd-numbered rnds.

NOTES
1) For this pattern, the colors in the O'Gos need to be separated (see page 2 for tips).

2) The wrap (yarn over) created by Sl1yo does not count as a separate stitch and should be treated as one stitch along with the slipped stitch it accompanies.

HAT
With A and larger circular needle, cast on 64 sts. Join in rnd, placing marker on first st.

1st to 8th rnds: *K1tbl. P1tbl. Rep from * around.

Change to smaller circular needle and proceed as follows in Stripe Pat:

Set up Brioche Pat: 1st rnd: With B, *K1. Sl1yo. Rep from * around.

2nd rnd: With E, *Sl1yo. BrP1. Rep from * around.

First rnd of Stripe Pat is now in position.

Keeping cont of Stripe Pat, proceed in Brioche Cable Pat as follows:

1st rnd: *BrK1. Sl1yo. BrDecR. Sl1yo. (BrK1. Sl1yo) 5 times. Rep from * around. 56 sts.

2nd rnd: *Sl1yo. BrP1. Rep from * around.

3rd rnd: *BrK1. Sl1yo. Rep from * around.

4th rnd: As 2nd rnd.

BRIOCHE CABLE HAT

5th rnd: *BrDecR. Sl1yo. (BrK1. yo. BrK1) all in next st. Sl1yo. (BrK1. Sl1yo) 5 times. Rep from * around.

6th rnd: *Sl1yo. BrP1. Sl1yo. P1. (Sl1yo. BrP1) 5 times. Rep from * around.

7th rnd: As 3rd rnd.

8th rnd: As 2nd rnd.

9th rnd: *BrK1. Sl1yo. (BrK1. yo. BrK1) all in next st. Sl1yo. (BrK1. Sl1yo) 5 times. Rep from * around. 64 sts.

10th rnd: As 6th rnd.

11th rnd: As 3rd rnd.

12th rnd: As 2nd rnd.

13th rnd: *(BrK1. Sl1yo) 5 times. BrDecR. Sl1yo. BrK1. Sl1yo. Rep from * around. 56 sts.

14th rnd: As 2nd rnd.

15th rnd: As 3rd rnd.

16th rnd: As 2nd rnd.

17th rnd: *(BrK1. Sl1yo) 4 times. Sl1yo. BrDecR. Sl1 yo. (BrK1. yo. BrK1) all in next st. Sl1yo. Rep from * around.

18th rnd: *(Sl1yo. BrP1) 5 times. Sl1yo. P1. Sl1yo. BrP1. Rep from * around.

19th rnd: As 3rd rnd.

20th rnd: As 2nd rnd.

21st rnd: *(BrK1. Sl1yo) 5 times. (BrK1. yo. BrK1) all in next st. Sl1yo. BrK1. Sl1yo. Rep from * around. 64 sts.

22nd rnd: *(Sl1yo. BrP1) 5 times. Sl1yo. P1. (Sl1yo. BrP1) twice. Rep from * around.

23rd rnd: As 3rd rnd.

24th rnd: As 2nd rnd.

These 24 rnds form Brioche Cable Pat.

Rep 1st to 22nd rnds of Brioche Cable Pat once more. Note: Change to set of 4 smaller needles during crown shaping as necessary.

SHAPE CROWN

1st rnd: *BrK1. Sl1yo. Rep from * around.

2nd and alt rnds: With E, *Sl1yo. BrP1. Rep from * around.

3rd rnd: *BrK1. Sl1yo. BrDecR. Sl1yo. (BrK1. Sl1yo) 5 times. Rep from * around. 56 sts.

5th rnd: *BrDecR. Sl1yo. (BrK1. Sl1yo) 5 times. Rep from * around. 48 sts.

7th rnd: *BrDecR. Sl1yo. (BrK1. Sl1yo) 4 times. Rep from * around. 40 sts.

9th rnd: *(BrK1. Sl1yo) twice. BrDecR. Sl1yo. BrK1. Sl1yo. Rep from * around. 32 sts.

11th rnd: *BrK1. Sl1yo. BrDecR. Sl1yo. BrK1. Sl1yo. Rep from * around. 24 sts.

12th rnd: As 2nd rnd.Break yarn, leaving a long end. Draw end tightly through rem 24 sts and fasten securely.

FINISHING

POMPOM

See diagrams on page 17. Wind A around 4 fingers approx 100 times. Remove from fingers and tie tightly in center. Cut through each side of loops. Trim to a smooth round shape. Sew pompom to top of Hat. •

Chart I: Brioche Cable

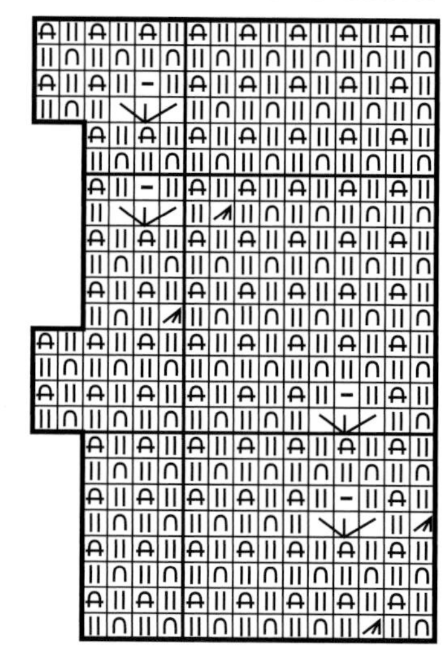

Key

- = BrDecR
- = BrK1
- = BrK1. yo. BrK1.
- = BrP1
- = Knit
- = Purl
- = Sl1yo

Chart II: Crown Shapin

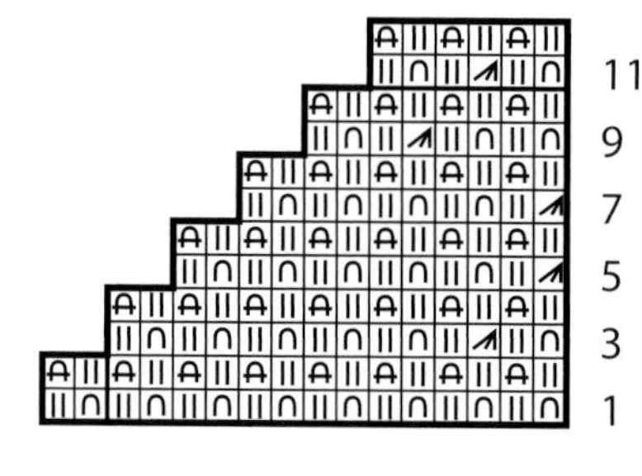

BEGINNER RIBBED & STRIPED COWL

Basic

MEASUREMENTS

Approx 18"/45.5cm tall x 28"/71cm around, unstretched.

MATERIALS

YARN

Caron® Big Donut™ O'Go™, 9.9oz/280g O'Gos, each approx 502yd/459m (acrylic) (4)

- 1 O'Go in #29008 Mint Julep (A)
- 1 O'Go in #29011 Boston Cream (B)

Note: 1 O'Go each of A and B makes 2 Cowls.

NEEDLES

- One size 8 (5mm) circular needle, 36"/91.5cm long, *or size needed to obtain gauge.*

NOTIONS

- Stitch marker
- Yarn needle

GAUGE

17 sts and 23 rows = 4"/10cm in St st.

TAKE TIME TO CHECK GAUGE.

STRIPE PAT

With A, work 2 rnds.

With B, work 2 rnds.

These 4 rnds form Stripe Pat.

COWL

With A, cast on 186 sts (multiple of 6 sts). Join in round (rnd). Place marker (PM) on first st.

1st rnd: *Knit 4 (K4). Purl 2 (P2). Repeat (rep) from * around.

First row of Stripe Pat is complete.

Keeping continuity (cont) of Stripe Pat, rep last rnd (K4. P2) ribbing until work from beginning (beg) measures approx 18"/45.5cm, ending with 2 rnds of A.

With A, cast off in ribbing. •

FADING STRIPES LUMBAR PILLOW

Basic

MEASUREMENTS

Approx 12"/30.5cm x 16"/40.5cm.

MATERIALS

YARN

Bernat® Blanket™ O'Go™, 10.5oz/300g O'Gos, each approx 220yd/201m (polyester)

- 1 O'Go in #42007 Shiraz (A, B, C)

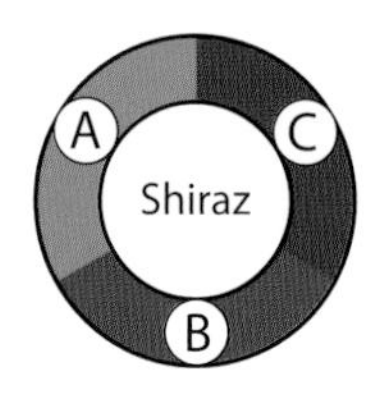

NEEDLES

- One size 11 (8mm) circular needle, 16"/40cm long, *or size needed to obtain gauge.*

NOTIONS

- Stitch marker
- Yarn needle
- 12"/30.5cm x 16"/40.5cm pillow form

GAUGE

8 sts and 13½ rnds = 4"/10cm in pat.

TAKE TIME TO CHECK GAUGE.

NOTES

1) For this pattern, the colors in the O'Go need to be separated (see page 2 for tips).

2) Pillow is worked in the round, from side to side, with 2 end seams. Place marker at beginning (beg) of rnd for easier counting.

STRIPE PAT

With A, work 9 rnds.

With B, work 9 rnds.

With C, work 18 rnds.

With B, work 9 rnds.

With A, work 9 rnds.

These 54 rnds form Stripe Pat.

PILLOW

With A, cast on 48 sts. Join for working in rnd, being careful not to twist and placing marker at first st.

1st rnd: Knit.

2nd rnd: Purl.

3rd and 4th rnds: Knit.

First 4 rnds of Stripe Pat are complete.

Keeping continuity (cont) of Stripe pat, repeat (rep) 2nd to 4th rnds 16 times more.

53rd rnd: With A, Purl.

54th rnd: Knit.

Bind off.

FINISHING

With A, sew cast on edge together (tog). Insert pillow form. With A, sew cast off edge tog. •

ADVENTUROUS BEGINNER BEANIE

Easy

SIZE

One size to fit Adult.

MATERIALS

YARN

Caron® Big Donut™ O'Go™, 9.9oz/280g O'Gos, each approx 502yd/459m (acrylic) (4)

• 1 O'Go in #29010 Choco-Blueberry (A, B, C, D, E)

Note: 1 O'Go makes 2 hats.

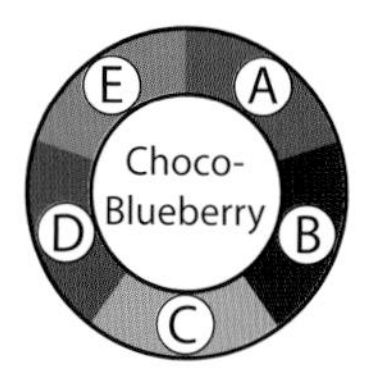

NEEDLES

• One size 8 (5mm) circular needle, 16"/40.5cm long, *or size needed to obtain gauge.*

• One set (5) double-pointed needles (dpn) size 8 (5mm), *or size needed to obtain gauge*

NOTIONS

• Yarn needle

• Stitch marker

GAUGE

17 sts and 23 rows = 4"/10cm in St st.

TAKE TIME TO CHECK GAUGE.

NOTES

1) For this pattern, the colors in the O'Go need to be separated (see page 2 for tips).

2) Hat is knit in St st in the round from bottom-up. Purl rnd creates fold line and hat edge. Inner brim is sewn to WS.

HAT

With circular needle and E, cast on 84 sts, leaving a 36"/91.5cm long end for seaming brim. Join in rnd, being careful not to twist. PM on first st.

INNER BRIM

Knit 12 rnds (St st).

SIDES

Next rnd: (Fold line). Purl.

Proceed as follows for RS of Hat:

Knit 2 rnds. Break E.

With B, knit 12 rnds. Break B.

With C, knit 12 rnds. Break C.

With D, knit 12 rnds. Break D.

With A, knit 3 rnds. Do not break A.

Note: Switch to set of 5 needles when necessary during shaping.

SHAPE CROWN

1st rnd: *K2tog. K10. ssk. Rep from * around. 72 sts.

2nd rnd and alt rnds: Knit.

3rd rnd: *ssk. K8. K2tog. Rep from * around. 60 sts.

5th rnd: *K2tog. K6. ssk. Rep from * around. 48 sts.

7th rnd: *K2tog. K4. ssk. Rep from * around. 36 sts.

9th rnd: *K2tog. K2. ssk. Rep from * around. 24 sts.

11th rnd: *K2tog. ssk. Rep from * around. 12 sts.

Break yarn, leaving a long end. Draw end through rem sts. Pull tightly. Fasten securely.

FINISHING

Fold brim along Fold line to WS and sew in position. •

RIBS & STRIPES YOKE SWEATER

Easy

SIZES

To fit bust measurement:

XS/S 28–34"/71–86.5cm

M 36–38"/91.5–96.5cm

L 40–42"/101.5–106.5cm

XL 44–46"/112–117cm

2/3XL 48–54"/122–137cm

4/5XL 56–62"/142–157.5cm

Finished bust:

XS/S 37"/94cm

M 41"/104cm

L 44"/112cm

XL 49"/124.5cm

2/3XL 58"/147.5cm

4/5XL 64"/162.5cm

MATERIALS

YARN

Caron® Colorama™ O'Go™, 6.4oz/180g O'Gos, each approx 228yd/208m (acrylic) (5)

- 1 (1, 1, 1, 1, 2, 2) O'Go in #68004 Lippy (A, B, C, D, E)
- 1 (1, 1, 1, 1, 2, 2) O'Go in #68021 Biker Jacket (F)
- 1 (1, 1, 1, 1, 2, 2) O'Go in #68022 Pave the Way (G)
- 1 (1, 1, 1, 1, 2, 2) O'Go in #68024 Sticky Rice (H)

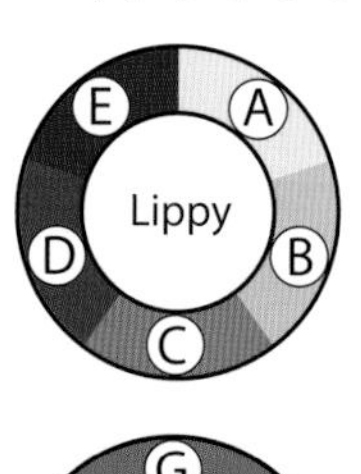

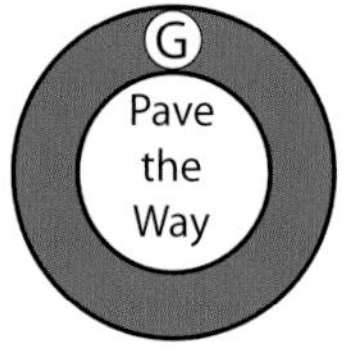

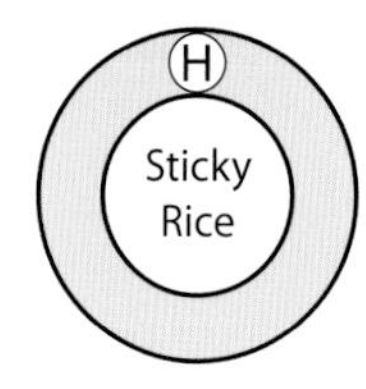

NEEDLES

- One size 10 (6mm) circular needle, 16"/40.5cm long, *or size needed to obtain gauge.*
- One size 10½ (6.5mm) circular needle, 16"/40cm long, *or size needed to obtain gauge.*
- One size 10 (6mm) circular needle, 29"/73.5cm long, *or size needed to obtain gauge.*
- One size 10½ (6.5mm) circular needle, 29"/73.5cm long, *or size needed to obtain gauge.*
- One set (4) double-pointed needles (dpn) size 10 (6mm), *or size needed to obtain gauge*
- One set (4) double-pointed needles (dpn) size 10½ (6.5mm), *or size needed to obtain gauge*

NOTIONS

- 2 stitch holders
- Stitch markers
- Yarn needle

GAUGE

12 sts and 18 rows = 4"/10cm with larger needles in St st.

TAKE TIME TO CHECK GAUGE.

STRIPE PAT I

Work 4 rnds of each color in the following sequence:

D, C, B, A, B, C, D and E.

These 32 rnds form Stripe Pat.

STRIPE PAT II

Purl 2 rnds of each color in the following sequence:

F, G, H and G.

These 8 rnds form Stripe Pat.

RIBS & STRIPES YOKE SWEATER

NOTES

1) Sweater is knit in one piece from top down.

2) The instructions are written for smallest size. If changes are necessary for larger size(s) the instructions will be written thus ( ). When only one number, it applies to all sizes.

3) For this pattern, the colors in the O'Gos need to be separated (see page 2 for tips).

4) For MC, work from O'Go with continuous color changing. To join next O'Go, match joining color.

BODY

NECKBAND

With smaller/short circular needle and E, cast on 44 (48-52-56-64-68) sts. Join in rnd. PM on first st.

1st rnd: *P1. K1. Rep from * around.

Rep last rnd of (K1. P1) ribbing for 3"/7.5cm.

Change to larger/short circular needle.

Proceed in Stripe Pat I, work Chart to end of chart, noting 4-st chart rep will be worked 11 (12-13-14-16-17) times. 165 (180-195-210-240-255) sts.

Note: Change to larger/long circular needle when necessary to accommodate all sts.

Next rnd: Pat 3 (0-6-0-0-0) sts. *M1P. Pat across 18 (15-27-21-30-51) sts. Rep from * around. 174 (192-202-220-248-260) sts.

Keeping cont of Stripe Pat I, purl next 7 (9-13-15-17-19) rnds.

DIVIDE FOR SLEEVES AND BODY

1st rnd: With appropriate color, P51 (58-61-68-80-86) for Back. Slip next 36 (38-40-42-44-44) sts for Left Sleeve onto a st holder. Cast on 4 (4-6-6-8-10) sts for underarm. P51 (58-61-68-80-86) for Front. Slip last 36 (38-40-42-44-44) sts for Right Sleeve onto a st holder. Cast on 4 (4-6-6-8-10) sts for underarm. Join in rnd. PM after 2nd (2nd-3rd-3rd-4th-5th) cast on sts. 110 (124-134-148-176-192) sts for Body. Stripe Pat I section is complete. Break yarn.

Join F and proceed in Stripe Pat II, purl in rnds (reverse Stockinette st) until Body from dividing rnd measures 13 (13-14½-14½-14-13)"/33 (33-37-37-35.5-33)cm. Break G and H.

Change to smaller/long circular needle and with F work 2"/5cm in (K1. P1) ribbing as given for neckband.
Cast off in ribbing.

SLEEVES

With larger set of double-pointed needles and F beg at underarm marker, pick up and knit 2 (2-3-3-4-5) sts. P36 (38-40-42-44-44) from st holder. Pick up and knit 2 (2-3-3-4-5) sts. Divide sts onto 3 needles. Join in rnd. PM for beg of rnd. 40 (42-46-48-52-54) sts.

First rnd of Stripe Pat II is complete.

Keeping cont of Stripe Pat II, purl 8 (8-5-5-6-6) rnds.

Dec 1 st at beg and end of next rnd and every following 12th (10th-9th-9th-7th-7th) rnd until there are 30 (30-32-34-36-38) sts.

Cont even in Stripe Pat II until Sleeve from pick up rnd measures 16 (16-16-16-14½-14½)"/40.5 (40.5-40.5-40.5-37-37)cm. Break G and H.

Change to smaller set of double-pointed needles and with F, work 2"/5cm in (K1. P1) ribbing as given for neckband. Cast off in ribbing. •

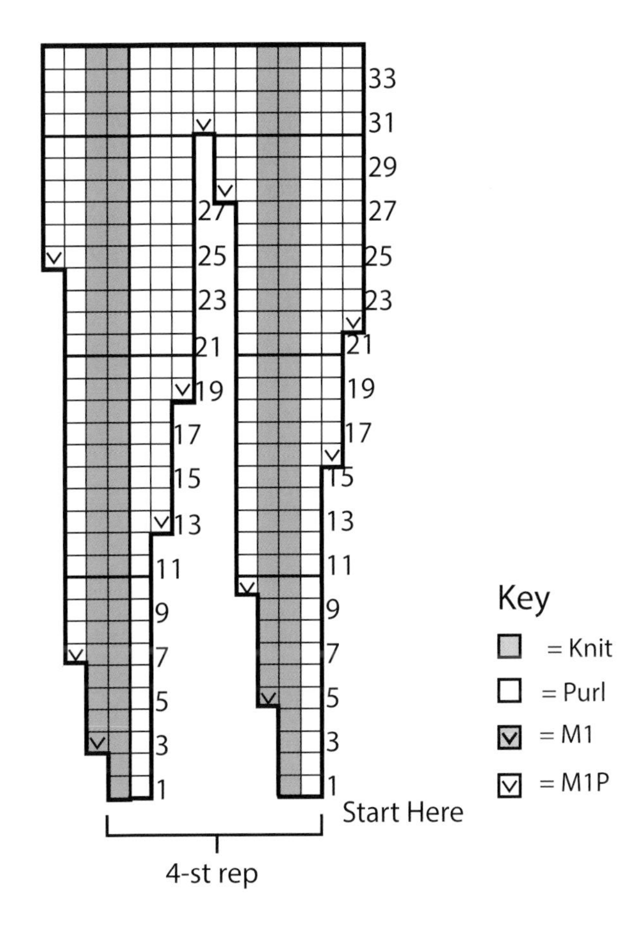

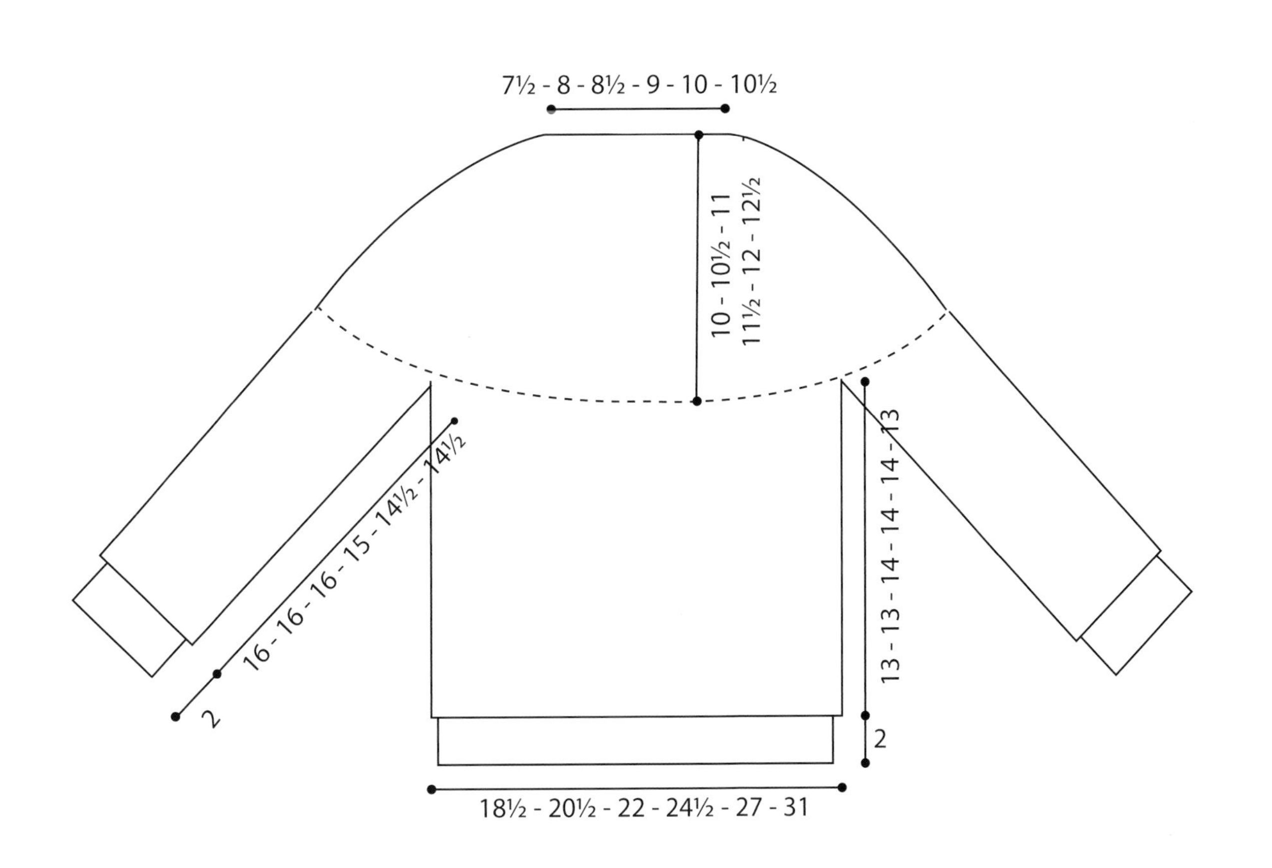

SAWTOOTH PANELS BLANKET

Easy

MEASUREMENTS

Approx 50"/127cm x 59"/150cm, excluding fringe.

MATERIALS

YARN

Caron® Big Donut™ O'Go™, 9.9oz/280g O'Gos, each approx 502yd/459m (acrylic)

- 3 O'Gos in #29007 Blue Velvet
- 3 O'Gos in #29002 Lemon Plum

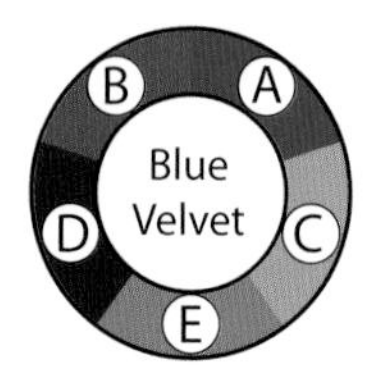

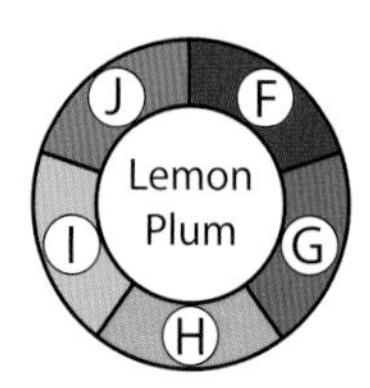

NEEDLES

- One pair size 8 (5mm) knitting needles, *or size needed to obtain gauge*

NOTIONS

- T-pins 1¾"/4.5cm long
- Yarn needle
- Size H/8 (5mm) crochet hook for fringe

GAUGE

16 sts and 30 rows = 4"/10cm in garter st.

TAKE TIME TO CHECK GAUGE.

STITCH GLOSSARY

W&T (Wrap and Turn) Bring yarn to front of work. Slip next stitch purlwise. Bring yarn to back of work. Slip stitch back onto left-hand needle. Turn.

NOTES

For this pattern, the colors in the O'Gos need to be separated (see page 2 for tips).

PANEL 1

FIRST TRIANGLE

With H, cast on 40 sts using 2 needle cable cast-on method.

1st row: (WS). With H, knit.

****2nd row:** (RS). K38. W&T.

Row 3 and alt (WS) rows: Knit.

4th row: K36. W&T.

6th row: K34. W&T.

8th row: K32. W&T.

10th row: K30. W&T.

12th row: K28. W&T.

14th row: K26. W&T.

16th row: K24. W&T.

18th row: K22. W&T.

20th row: K20. W&T.

22nd row: K18. W&T.

24th row: K16. W&T.

26th row: K14. W&T.

28th row: K12. W&T.

30th row: K10. W&T.

32nd row: K8. W&T.

34th row: K6. W&T.

36th row: K4. W&T.

38th row: K2. W&T.

39th row: (WS). Knit. Break H. Join E.

SECOND TRIANGLE

1st row: (RS). With E, knit across all sts (you do not have to pick up and knit the wraps, just knit as you normally would).

2nd row: K38. W&T.

SAWTOOTH PANELS BLANKET

Row 3 and alt (RS) rows: Knit.

4th row: K36. W&T.

6th row: K34. W&T.

8th row: K32. W&T.

10th row: K30. W&T.

12th row: K28. W&T.

14th row: K26. W&T.

16th row: K24. W&T.

18th row: K22. W&T.

20th row: K20. W&T.

22nd row: K18. W&T.

24th row: K16. W&T.

26th row: K14. W&T.

28th row: K12. W&T.

30th row: K10. W&T.

32nd row: K8. W&T.

34th row: K6. W&T.

36th row: K4. W&T.

38th row: K2. W&T.

40th row: (WS). Knit across all sts (you do not have to pick up and knit the wraps, just knit as you normally would). Break E. Join H.**

Rep from ** to ** 10 times more (22 Triangles).

With E, cast off all sts.

PANEL 2

FIRST TRIANGLE

With G, cast on 40 sts using 2 needle cable cast-on method.

****1st row:** (WS). K38. W&T.

Row 2 and alt (RS) rows: Knit.

3rd row: K36. W&T.

5th row: K34. W&T.

7th row: K32. W&T.

9th row: K30. W&T.

11th row: K28. W&T.

13th row: K26. W&T.

15th row: K24. W&T.

17th row: K22. W&T.

19th row: K20. W&T.

21st row: K18. W&T.

23rd row: K16. W&T.

25th row: K14. W&T.

27th row: K12. W&T.

29th row: K10. W&T.

31st row: K8. W&T.

33rd row: K6. W&T.

35th row: K4. W&T.

37th row: K2. W&T.

39th row: (WS). Knit across all sts (you do not have to pick up and knit the wraps, just knit as you normally would). Break G. Join C.**

SECOND TRIANGLE

1st row: (RS). With C, K38. W&T.

Row 2 and alt (WS) rows: Knit.

3rd row: K36. W&T.

5th row: K34. W&T.

7th row: K32. W&T.

9th row: K30. W&T.

11th row: K28. W&T.

13th row: K26. W&T.

15th row: K24. W&T.

17th row: K22. W&T.

19th row: K20. W&T.

21st row: K18. W&T.

23rd row: K16. W&T.

25th row: K14. W&T.

27th row: K12. W&T.

29th row: K10. W&T.

31st row: K8. W&T.

33rd row: K6. W&T.

35th row: K4. W&T.

37th row: K2. W&T.

38th row: (WS). Knit. *** Break C. Join G.

39th row: (RS). With G, knit across all sts (you do not have to pick up and knit the wraps, just knit as you normally would).**

Rep from ** to ** 9 times more, then from ** to ** once. (22 Triangles).
With C, cast off all sts.

PANEL 3

Work as for Panel 1, substituting J for H and B for E.

PANEL 4

Work as for Panel 2, substituting I for G and A for C.

PANEL 5

Work as for Panel 1, substituting F for H and D for E.

FINISHING

Block each Panel into rectangles measuring approx. 9½"/24cm wide x 55"/139.5cm long.
Pin Panels tog, taking care to match sides of Triangles, lining up cast on edge across bottoms and blocking/ adjusting Panels to straighten as needed. Sew tog with flat seam in this order: Panel 1, 2, 3, 4, 5.

FRINGE

See fringe diagram on page 52. Cut 68 lengths of each color 15"/38cm long. Using contrasting shade to match Panel at each end, taking 4 strands tog, knot into fringe, spacing 17 fringes evenly across end of each Panel. Trim fringe evenly. •

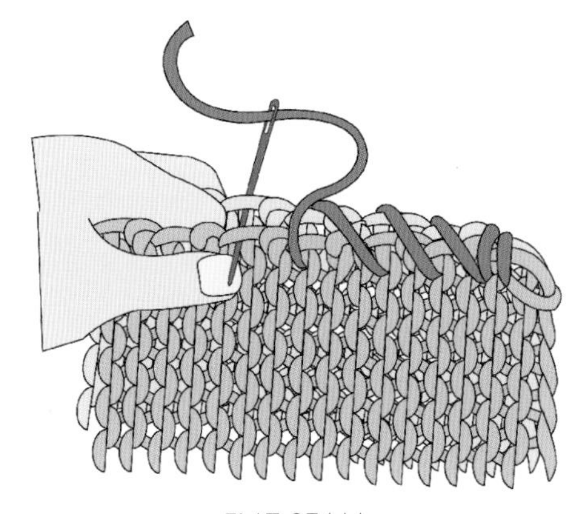

FLAT SEAM

FADING SHADES HAT

Basic

SIZE

One size to fit Adult.

MATERIALS

YARN

Caron® Colorama™ O'Go™, 6.4oz/180g O'Gos, each approx 228yd/208m (acrylic) (5)

• 1 O'Go in #68004 Lippy or #68015 Blue Mustang (A, B, C, D, E)

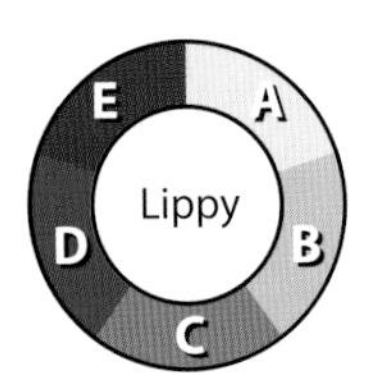

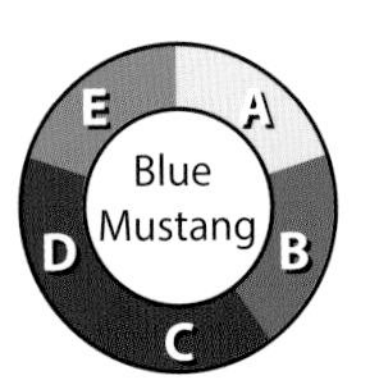

NEEDLES

• One set (4) double-pointed needles (dpn) size 9 (5.5mm), *or size needed to obtain gauge*

• One set (4) double-pointed needles (dpn) size 10 (6mm), *or size needed to obtain gauge*

NOTIONS

• Stitch marker

• Yarn needle

GAUGE

13 sts and 18 rows = 4"/10cm in St st using larger needles.

TAKE TIME TO CHECK GAUGE.

NOTES

For this pattern, the colors in the O'Go need to be separated (see page 2 for tips).

HAT

With smaller set of needles and A, cast on 68 sts. Divide sts on 3 needles (24 sts on first 2 needles and 20 sts on 3rd needle). Join in rnd, placing marker on first st.

1st rnd: *K2. P2. Rep from * around.

Rep last rnd (K2. P2) ribbing for 2"/5cm

Change to larger set of needles and knit next rnd.

First rnd of Chart is complete.

Knit Chart to end of chart, reading rnds from right to left and noting 2-st rep will be worked 34 times.

SHAPE TOP

1st rnd: With E, *K15. K2tog. Rep from * around. 64 sts.

2nd rnd: *K6. K2tog. Rep from * around. 56 sts.

3rd rnd: *K5. K2tog. Rep from * around. 48 sts.

4th rnd: *K4. K2tog. Rep from * around. 40 sts.

5th rnd: *K3. K2tog. Rep from * around. 32 sts.

6th rnd: *K2. K2tog. Rep from * around. 24 sts.

7th rnd: *K1. K2tog. Rep from * around. 16 sts.

8th rnd: (K2tog) 8 times. 8 sts.

Break yarn leaving a long end. Draw end tightly through rem sts and fasten securely.

FINISHING

POMPOM

See diagrams on page 17. With 1 strand each of A, B, C, D, and E held tog, wind yarn around 4 fingers 30 times. Remove from fingers and tie tightly in center. Cut through each side of loops. Trim to a smooth round shape. Sew to top of Hat. •

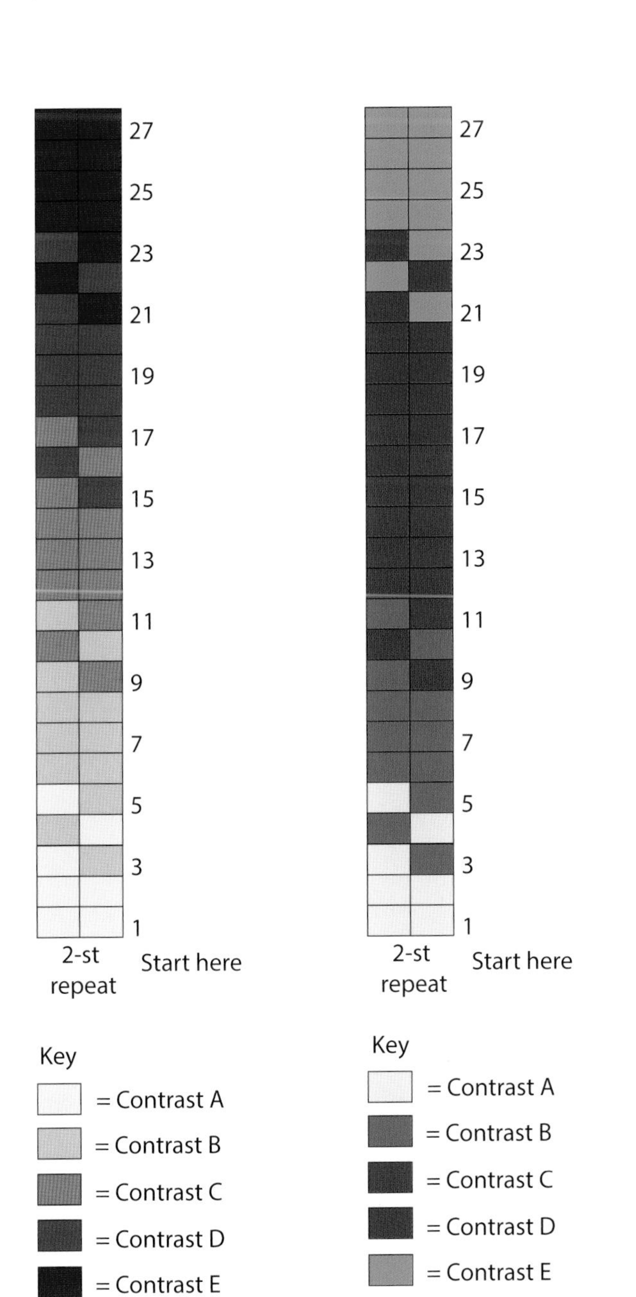

BRIOCHE SCARF

Basic

MEASUREMENTS
Approx 8"/20.5cm wide x 70"/178cm long.

MATERIALS
YARN

Caron® Colorama™ O'Go™, 6.4oz/180g O'Gos, each approx 228yd/208m (acrylic) (5)

- 1 O'Go in #68013 Baja (A)
- 1 O'Go in #68009 First Blush (B)

NEEDLES

- One size 10½ (6.5mm) circular needle, 16"/40cm long, *or size needed to obtain gauge.*

NOTION

- Yarn needle

GAUGE
12 sts and 32 rows = 4"/10cm in Brioche Pat.

TAKE TIME TO CHECK GAUGE.

STITCH GLOSSARY
Sl3Pwyif Slip next 3 stitches purlwise, with yarn in front.

See inside back cover for instructions for brioche techniques.

NOTES
1) The wrap (yarn over) created by Sl1yo does not count as a separate stitch and should be treated as 1 stitch along with slipped stitch it accompanies.

2) The last 3 sts of each row are slipped purlwise, with yarn in front to create an I-cord edging.

SCARF
With A, cast on 31 sts. Do not join. Work back and forth across needle.

Set-up row: (RS). With A, K3. *Sl1yo. K1. Rep from * to last 4 sts. Sl1yo. Sl3Pwyif. Do not turn. Slide sts to other end of needle.

1st row: (RS). With B, K3. *BrP1. Sl1yo. Rep from * to last 4 sts. BrP1. Sl3Pwyif. Turn.

2nd row: (WS). With A, K3. *Sl1yo. BrP1. Rep from * to last 4 sts. Sl1yo. Sl3Pwyif. Do not turn. Slide sts to other end of needle.

3rd row: (WS). With B, K3. *BrK1. Sl1yo. Rep from * to last 4 sts. BrK1. Sl3Pwyif. Turn.

4th row: (RS). With A, K3. *Sl1yo. BrK1. Rep from * to last 4 sts. Sl1yo. Sl3Pwyif.

Rep 1st to 4th rows for Brioche Pat until work from beg measures approx 70"/178cm, ending on a 2nd or 4th row of pat.

Next row: (Cast off row). With A, cast off, treating each yo as 1 st along with its accompanying slipped st. •

THE RIGHT STRIPE SWEATER

Easy

SIZES

To fit bust measurement:

XS/S 28–34"/71–86.5cm

M 36–38"/91.5–96.5cm

L 40–42"/101.5–106.5cm

XL 44–46"/112–117cm

2/3XL 48–54"/122–137cm

4/5XL 56–62"/142–157.5cm

Finished bust:

XS 44"/112cm

M 48"/122cm

L 52"/132cm

XL 56"/142cm

2/3XL 63"/160cm

4/5XL 69"/175.5cm

MATERIALS

YARN

Caron® Big Donut™ O'Go™, 9.9oz/280g O'Gos, each approx 502yd/459m (acrylic) (4)

- 5 (6, 7, 7, 8, 9) O'Gos in #29001 Spiced Ginger (A, B, C, D, E)

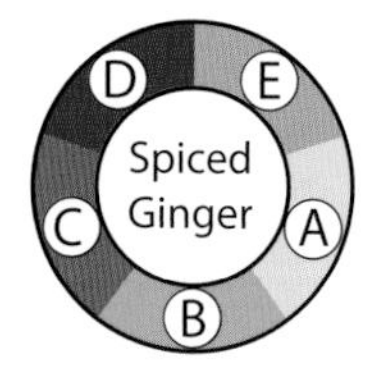

NEEDLES

- One pair size 7 (4.5mm) knitting needles, *or size needed to obtain gauge*
- One pair size 8 (5mm) knitting needles, or size needed to obtain gauge

NOTIONS

- 4 stitch markers
- 2 stitch holders
- Yarn needle

GAUGE

17 sts and 23 rows = 4"/10cm in St st with larger needles.

TAKE TIME TO CHECK GAUGE.

STRIPE PAT I (WORKED IN ST ST)

With D, work 4"/10cm, ending on a purl row.

With E, work 1"/2.5cm ending on a purl row.

With C, work 4"/10cm ending on a purl row.

With E, work 1"/2.5cm ending on a purl row.

With B, work 4"/10cm ending on a purl row.

With E, work 1"/2.5cm ending on a purl row.

With A, work 4"/10cm ending on a purl row.

These 19"/48cm form Stripe Pat I.

STRIPE PAT II (WORKED IN ST ST)

With A, work 2"/5cm, ending on a purl row.

With E, work 2"/5cm, ending on a purl row.

These 4"/10cm form Stripe Pat II.

STRIPE PAT III (WORKED IN ST ST)

With B work 2"/5cm, ending on a purl row.

With C work 2"/5cm, ending on a purl row.

These 4"/10cm form Stripe Pat III.

NOTES

1) The instructions are written for smallest size. If changes are necessary for larger size(s) the instructions will be written thus ( ). When only one number, it applies to all sizes.

THE RIGHT STRIPE SWEATER

2) For this pattern, the colors in the O'Gos need to be separated (see page 2 for tips).

BACK

**With smaller needles and D, cast on cast on 90 (102-110-118-134-146) sts.

1st row: *K2. P2. Rep from * to last 2 sts. K2.

2nd row: *P2. K2. Rep from * to last 2 sts. P2.

Rep last 2 rows of (K2. P2) ribbing 8 times more. Break D.**

Change to larger needles and work Stripe Pat I until piece from beg measures 22 (22½-24-24-25½-26)"/56 (57-61-61-65-66)cm, ending on a purl row.

With A, proceed as follows:

SHAPE SHOULDERS

Cast off 7 (8-9-10-12-13) sts beg next 6 rows, then 7 (9-9-10-10-13) sts beg next 2 rows. Leave rem 34 (36-38-38-42-42) sts on a st holder.

FRONT

Work from ** to ** as given for Back.

Change to larger needles and work Stripe Pat I until piece from beg measures 20 (20½-22-22-23½-24)"/51 (52-56-56-58.5-61)cm, ending on a purl row.

SHAPE LEFT NECK

Next row: (RS). K31 (36-39-43-49-55). K2tog (neck edge). Turn. Leave rem sts unworked.

Cont on 32 (37-40-44-50-56) sts.

Next row: Purl.

Next row: Knit to last 2 sts. K2tog.

Next row: Purl.

Rep last 2 rows 3 times more. 28 (33-36-40-46-52) sts rem.

With A only, proceed as follows:

SHAPE SHOULDER

Next row: (RS). Cast off 7 (8-9-10-12-13) sts. Knit to end of row.

Next row: Purl.

Rep last 2 rows once more.

Next row: Cast off 7 (8-9-10-12-13) sts. Knit to end of row.

Next row: Purl.

Cast off rem 7 (9-9-10-10-13) sts.

With RS facing, slip next 24 (26-28-28-32-32) sts onto a st holder for front neck.

Join A to rem sts and proceed as follows:

SHAPE RIGHT NECK

Next row: (RS). ssk. Knit to end of row. 32 (37-40-44-50-56) sts.

Next row: Purl.

Rep last 2 rows until there are 28 (33-36-40-46-52) sts, ending on a knit row.

SHAPE SHOULDER

Next row: (WS). Cast off 7 (8-9-10-12-13) sts. Purl to end of row.

Next row: Knit.

Rep last 2 rows once more.

Next row: Cast off 7 (8-9-10-12-13) sts. Purl to end of row.

Knit 1 row.

Cast off rem 7 (9-9-10-10-13) sts.

SLEEVES

Note: Make Left Sleeve using Stripe Pat II and Right Sleeve using Stripe Pat III.

With smaller needles and D, cast on 34 (34-42-42-50-50) sts.

Work 2"/5cm in (K2. P2) ribbing as given for Back, ending on a WS row and inc 2 sts evenly across last row. 36 (36-44-44-52-52) sts.

Change to larger needles and beg working Stripe Pat II or III (see note) for 4 rows.

Keeping cont of Stripe Pat, inc 1 st each end of next and following 4th rows until there are 76 (80-84-84-86-92) sts.

Keeping cont of Stripe Pat, work even in St st until piece from beg measures 18 (17½-17-17-16½-15½)"/45.5 (44.5-43-43-40.5-39.5)cm, ending on a purl row.

Bind off.

FINISHING

Pin pieces to measurements. Cover with a damp cloth, leaving cloth to dry. Sew right shoulder seam, leaving left shoulder seam open.

NECKBAND

With RS facing, smaller needles and A, pick up and knit 12 sts down left front neck edge. K24 (26-28-28-32-32) from front neck st holder. Pick up and knit 12 sts up right front neck edge. K34 (36-38-38-42-42) from Back neck st holder. 82 (86-90-90-98-98) sts.

1st row: (WS). *P2. K2. Rep from * to last 2 sts. P2.

2nd row: *K2. P2. Rep from * to last 2 sts. K2.

Rep last 2 rows of (K2. P2) ribbing twice more.

Cast off in ribbing.

Sew left shoulder and neckband seam. Place markers on side edges of Front and Back 9 (9½-10-10-10½-11)"/23 (24-25.5-25.5-26.5-28)cm down from shoulders.

Sew cast off edge of sleeves between markers on body.

Sew side and sleeve seams. •

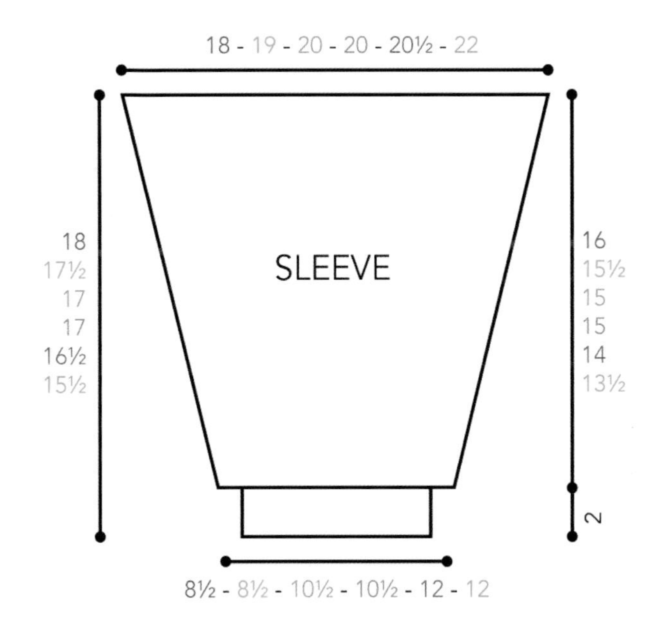

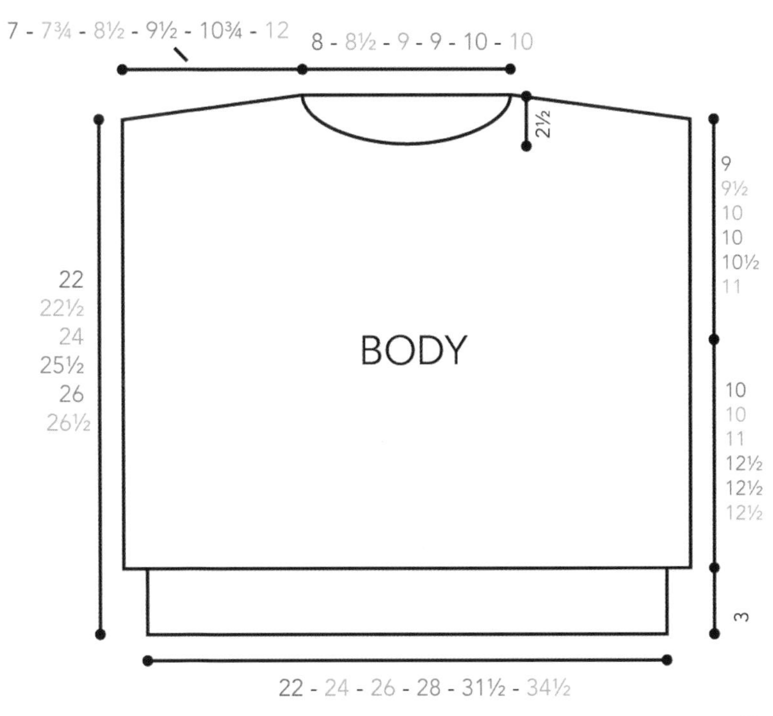

ON THE GO KNIT HAT

Easy

SIZE

One size to fit Adult head.

MATERIALS

YARN

Caron® Colorama™ O'Go™, 6.4oz/180g O'Gos, each approx 228yd/208m (acrylic) (5)

• 1 O'Go in #68013 Baja

Note: 1 O'Go will make 2 Hats.

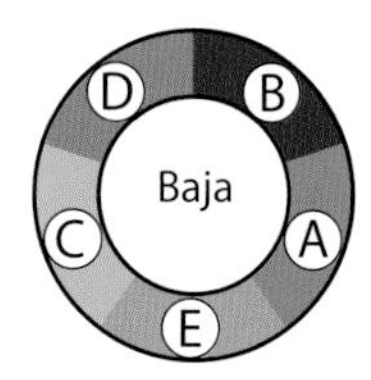

NEEDLES

• One size 10½ (6.5mm) circular needle, 16"/40cm long, *or size needed to obtain gauge*

• One set (4) double-pointed needles (dpn) size 10½ (6.5mm), *or size needed to obtain gauge*

VERSION 1

GAUGE

12 sts and 17 rows = 4"/10cm in St st.

TAKE TIME TO CHECK GAUGE.

NOTES

1) For this pattern, the colors in the O'Go need to be separated (see page 2 for tips).

2) If you would like to make both Hats from 1 O'Go, knit Version I first then use leftover yarn in any order to knit Version II.

3) If making Version II from a separate O'Go, use working tail from either end of O'Go and do no separate shades.

VERSION I

With circular needle and B, cast on 64 sts. Join in rnd.

1st and 2nd rnds: *K1. P1. Rep from * around. Join E.

With E, rep last rnd of (K1. P1) ribbing until work from beg measures 4"/10cm. Join A.

With A, rep last rnd of (K1. P1) ribbing until work from beg measures 5"/12.5cm.

Proceed in pat as follows:

1st rnd: With A, *K3. K1 wrapping yarn twice around needle. Rep from * around.

2nd rnd: *K3. Sl1Pwyib, dropping extra loop. Rep from * around.

3rd and 4th rnds: *K3. Sl1Pwyib. Rep from * around.

Last 4 rnds form pat.

Keeping cont of pat, With A, work 6 rows.

With B, work 2 rows.

With C, work 10 rows.

With B, work 2 rows.

SHAPE TOP

1st rnd: With D, *K2tog. K1. K1 wrapping yarn twice

around needle. Rep from * around. 48 sts.

2nd rnd: *K2. Sl1Pwyib, dropping extra loop. Rep from * around.

3rd and 4th rnds: *K2. Sl1Pwyib. Rep from * around.

5th rnd: *K2tog. K1 wrapping yarn twice around needle. Rep from * around. 32 sts.

6th rnd: *K1. Sl1Pwyib, dropping extra loop. Rep from * around.

7th and 8th rnds: *K1. Sl1Pwyib. Rep from * around.

9th rnd: (K2tog) 16 times. 16 sts.

Break yarn, leaving long end. Thread end through rem sts. Pull tightly. Fasten securely.

FINISHING

Fold ribbing 3"/7.5cm to RS for brim.

POMPOM

Wind B around 4 fingers 80 times. Tie tightly in the middle and leave a long end for attaching to Hat. Cut loops at both ends and trim to smooth round shape. Sew securely to top of Hat.

VERSION II

With circular needle, cast on 64 sts. Join in rnd.

1st rnd: *K1. P1. Rep from * around.

Rep last rnd of (K1. P1) ribbing until work from beg measures 5"/12.5cm.

Proceed in pat as follows:

1st rnd: *K3. K1 wrapping yarn twice around needle. Rep from * around.

2nd rnd: *K3. Sl1Pwyib, dropping extra loop. Rep from * around.

3rd and 4th rnds: *K3. Sl1Pwyib. Rep from * around.

Rep last 4 rnds of pat until work from beg measures 9"/23cm.

SHAPE TOP

1st rnd: *K2tog. K1. K1 wrapping yarn twice around needle. Rep from * around. 48 sts.

2nd rnd: *K2. Sl1Pwyib, dropping extra loop. Rep from * around.

3rd and 4th rnds: *K2. Sl1Pwyib. Rep from * around.

5th rnd: *K2tog. K1 wrapping yarn twice around needle. Rep from * around. 32 sts.

6th rnd: *K1. Sl1Pwyib, dropping extra loop. Rep from * around.

7th and 8th rnds: *K1. Sl1Pwyib. Rep from * around.

9th rnd: (K2tog) 16 times. 16 sts.

Break yarn, leaving long end. Thread end through rem sts. Pull tightly. Fasten securely.

FINISHING

See Version I finishing instructions. •

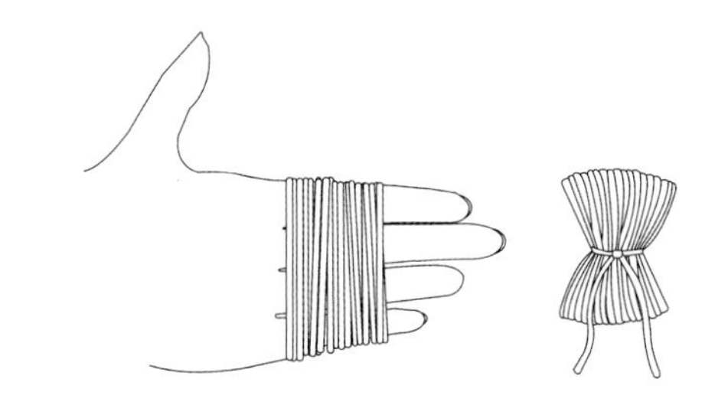

VERSION 2

FENANGLE THE ANGLES BLANKET SCARF

Basic

MEASUREMENTS

Approx 22"/56cm x 77"/195.5cm, excluding fringe.

MATERIALS

YARN

Caron® Colorama™ O'Go™, 6.4oz/180g O'Gos, each approx 228yd/208m (acrylic)

- 2 O'Gos in #68004 Lippy (A, B, C, D, E)
- 2 O'Gos in #68009 First Blush (A, B, F, G, H)
- 2 O'Gos in #68013 Baja (I, J, K, L, M)

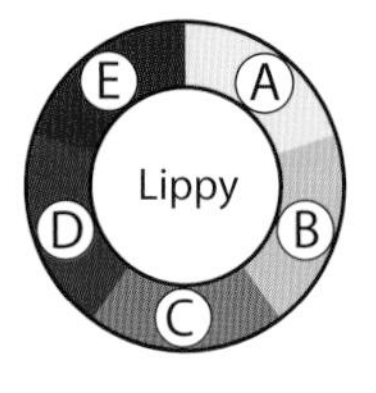

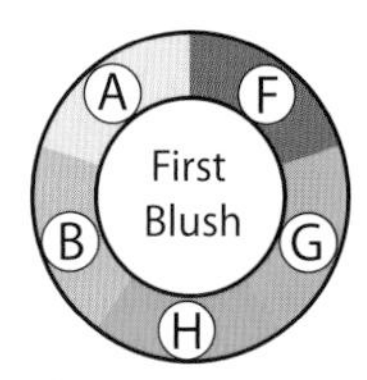

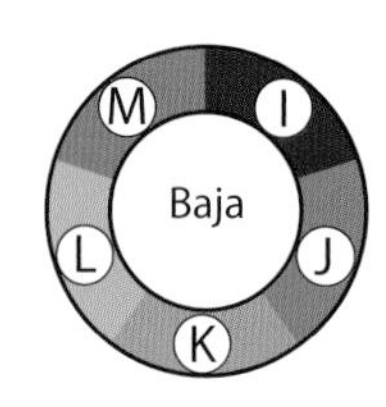

NEEDLES

- One pair size 10 (6mm) knitting needles, *or size needed to obtain gauge*

NOTION

- Yarn needle

GAUGE

12 sts and 26 rows = 4"/10cm in garter st.

Block = Approx 11"/29cm square.

TAKE TIME TO CHECK GAUGE.

STITCH GLOSSARY

W&T (Wrap and Turn) Bring yarn to front of work. Slip next stitch purlwise. Bring yarn to back of work. Slip stitch back onto left-hand needle. Turn. (See diagrams on page 52.)

NOTES

1) For this pattern, the colors in the O'Go need to be separated (see page 2 for tips).

2) Contrast A and B appear in both Lippy and First Blush.

3) Leave long tail at beg of cast on of Block 1 and end of cast off for Blocks 3, 5, 7, 9, and 11 to sew seams when Scarf is complete.

COLOR PLACEMENT

(See Color Placement Diagram on page 50.)

BLOCK 1
Color 1: L
Color 2: D
Color 3: B
Color 4: F

BLOCK 2
Color 1: E
Color 2: B
Color 3: M
Color 4: I

BLOCK 3
Color 1: C
Color 2: B
Color 3: F
Color 4: A

BLOCK 4
Color 1: D
Color 2: G
Color 3: K
Color 4: A

BLOCK 5
Color 1: B
Color 2: M
Color 3: C
Color 4: K

BLOCK 6
Color 1: A
Color 2: E
Color 3: H
Color 4: J

FENANGLE THE ANGLES BLANKET SCARF

BLOCK 7

Color 1: L

Color 2: D

Color 3: G

Color 4: J

BLOCK 8

Color 1: I

Color 2: H

Color 3: F

Color 4: L

BLOCK 9

Color 1: B

Color 2: J

Color 3: H

Color 4: K

BLOCK 10

Color 1: I

Color 2: H

Color 3: A

Color 4: M

BLOCK 11

Color 1: G

Color 2: C

Color 3: K

Color 4: I

BLOCK 12

Color 1: L

Color 2: C

Color 3: B

Color 4: E

BLOCK 13

Color 1: J

Color 2: F

Color 3: B

Color 4: G

BLOCK 14

Color 1: D

Color 2: M

Color 3: B

Color 4: E

Color Placement Diagram

BLOCK 1

TRIANGLE 1

With Color 1, cast on 33 sts.

1st row: (RS). Knit.

2nd row: K31. W&T.

3rd row: Knit.

4th row: Knit to 2 sts before last wrapped st. W&T.

5th row: Knit.

Rep last 2 rows until 3 sts rem.

Next row: (WS). K1. W&T.

Next row: K1.

Next row: K33.

Break color 1.

TRIANGLE 2

With Color 2, proceed as follows:

1st row: (RS). Knit.

2nd row: Knit.

3rd row: K1. W&T.

4th row: Knit.

5th row: Knit to 1 st after last wrapped st. W&T.

6th row: Knit.

Rep last 2 rows until 1 st rem after wrapped st and last row is K31.

(1 st remains unworked after last wrapped st. 1st row of next Triangle is worked across all 33 sts)

Break Color 2.

TRIANGLE 3

With Color 3, as Triangle 1. Break Color 3.

TRIANGLE 4

With Color 4, as Triangle 2. Cast off purl-wise at end of last row. **

BLOCK 2

With RS facing and Color 1 as indicated for current Block, pick up and knit 33 sts evenly along left side edge of Block 1.

Work from ** to ** as given for Block 1.

BLOCKS 3–14

Work all following Blocks as given for Block 2, picking up sts for 1st row along left or right side of previous Block as indicated below:

(See Color Placement Diagram on page 50.)

Block 3: Pick up 33 sts along right side of Block 2.

Block 4: Pick up 33 sts along right side of Block 3.

Block 5: Pick up 33 sts along left side of Block 4.

Block 6: Pick up 33 sts along left side of Block 5.

Block 7: Pick up 33 sts along right side of Block 6.

Block 8: Pick up 33 sts along right side of Block 7.

Block 9: Pick up 33 sts along left side of Block 8.

FENANGLE THE ANGLES BLANKET SCARF

Block 10: Pick up 33 sts along left side of Block 9.

Block 11: Pick up 33 sts along right side of Block 10.

Block 12: Pick up 33 sts along right side of Block 11.

Block 13: Pick up 33 sts along left side of Block 12.

Block 14: Pick up 33 sts along left side of Block 13.

Assembly Diagram

Block 1 ▼	Block 2 ▶
Block 4 ◀	Block 3 ▼
Block 5 ▼	Block 6 ▶
Block 8 ◀	Block 7 ▼
Block 9 ▼	Block 10 ▶
Block 12 ◀	Block 11 ▼
Block 13 ▼	Block 14 ▶

FINISHING

Pin Scarf to measurements. Cover with a damp cloth, leaving cloth to dry.

Sew seams between Blocks as shown in Assembly Diagram using a flat seam.

FRINGE

Cut lengths of A, 20"/51cm long. Taking 2 strands tog, knot into fringe into evenly across each short end of Scarf. Trim fringe evenly. •

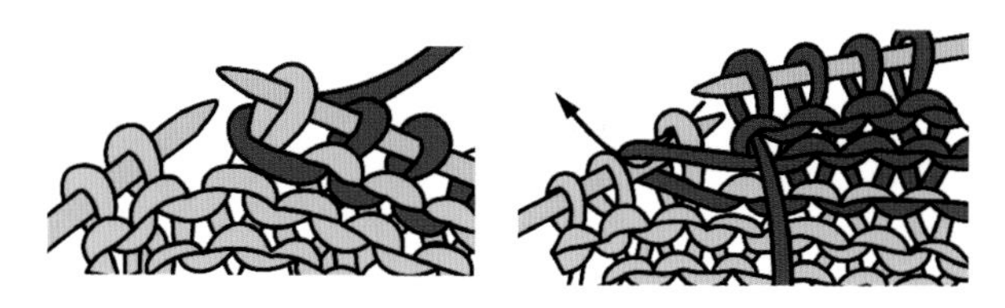

WRAP & TURN

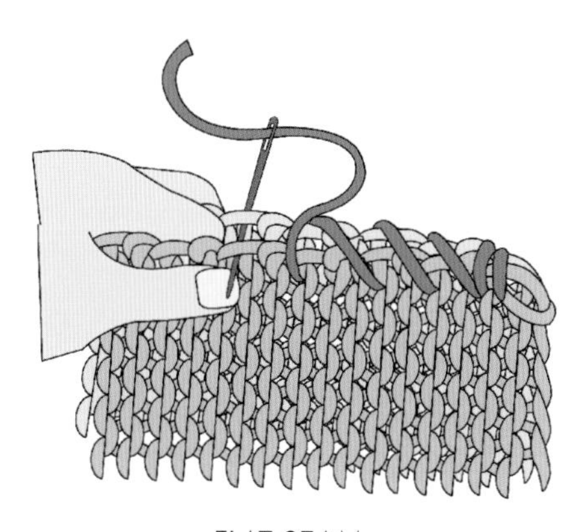

FLAT SEAM

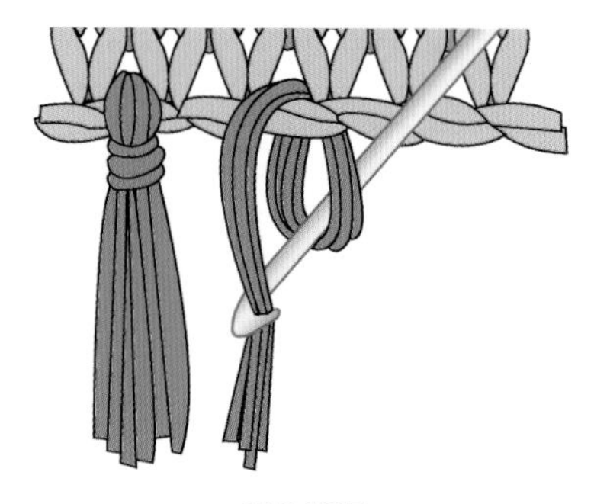

FRINGE

BRIGHT SIDE COWL

Basic

MEASUREMENTS

Approx 13½"/34cm tall x 24"/61cm in diameter.

MATERIALS

YARN

Caron® Colorama™ O'Go™, 6.4oz/180g O'Gos, each approx 228yd/208m (acrylic) (5)

- 1 O'Go in #68015 Blue Mustang

NEEDLES

- One pair size 10 (6mm) knitting needles, *or size needed to obtain gauge*

NOTION

- Yarn needle

GAUGE

13 sts and 18 rows = 4"/10cm in St st.

TAKE TIME TO CHECK GAUGE.

NOTES

1) Cowl is knit sideways.

2) There is no right or wrong side. Cowl is reversible.

COWL

Cast on 44 sts.

1st to 10th rows: Sl1P. Knit to end of row.

11th to 18th rows: Sl1P. P1. *K1. P1. Rep from * to end of row.

Rep last 18 rows for pat until work from beg measures approx 24"/61cm ending on an 18th row.

Bind off.

FINISHING

Sew cast on and cast off edges tog using flat seam (see diagram on page 52) to form Cowl. •

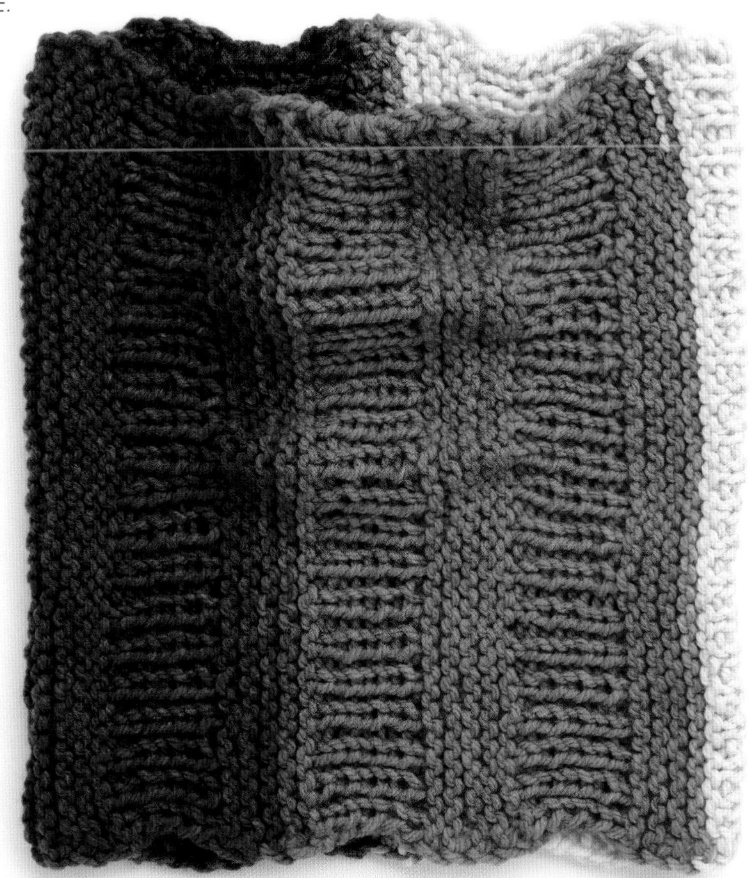

EASY STRIPED & BLOCKED HAT

Easy

SIZE

One size to fit Adult.

MATERIALS

YARN

Caron® Colorama™ O'Go™, 6.4oz/180g O'Gos, each approx 228yd/208m (acrylic) (5)

- 1 O'Go in #68013 Baja

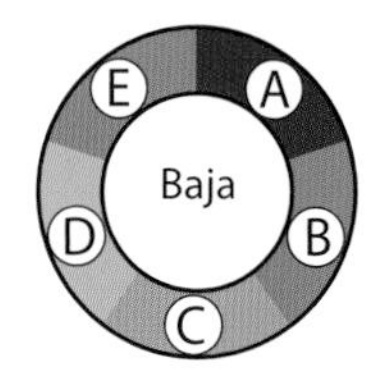

NEEDLES

- One pair size 10 (6mm) knitting needles, *or size needed to obtain gauge*

NOTION

- Yarn needle

GAUGE

13 sts and 18 rows = 4"/10cm in St st.

TAKE TIME TO CHECK GAUGE.

STRIPE PAT (WORKED IN ST ST)

With C, work 2 rows.

With D, work 2 rows.

With B, work 2 rows.

With A, work 2 rows.

These 8 rows form Stripe Pat.

NOTES

1) For this pattern, the colors in the O'Go need to be separated (see page 2 for tips).

2) To change colors within each row, wrap the 2 colors around each other where they meet on WS to avoid a hole.

3) When working Stripe Pat, carry colors loosely up WS of work.

HAT

LOWER EDGING

With A, cast on 60 sts.

Beg on a knit row, work 4 rows St st.

Next row: (WS – fold line). Knit.

Beg on a knit row, work 4 rows St st.

Next row: (RS – joining row). *Pick up next st from cast on edge. K2tog with next st on needle. Rep from * to end of row, creating folded lower edge.

Next row: (WS). (K16. Kfb) twice. Knit to end of row. 62 sts.

Proceed in Color Block Pat as follows:

1st row: (RS). With C, K31 (1st row of Stripe Pat). With E, K31.

2nd row: With E, P31. With C, P31 (2nd row of Stripe Pat).
Color Block and Stripe Pat is now in position.

Work a further 20 rows in Color Block and Stripe Pat, ending on a purl row.

Next row: (RS). With A, knit across all sts.
Next row: With A, purl across all sts.
Next row: With E, K31. With C, K31 (1st row of Stripe Pat).
Next row: With C, P31 (2nd row of Stripe Pat). With E, P31.
Color Block and Stripe Pat is now in position.

Work a further 6 rows in Color Block and Stripe Pat, ending on a purl row.

SHAPE TOP
1st row: (RS). With E, K1. K2tog. (K5. K2tog) 4 times. With C, (K5. K2tog) 4 times. K2tog. K1. 52 sts.
2nd row: With C, P26. With E, P26.
3rd row: With E, K26. With D, K26.
4th row: With D, P26. With E, P26.
5th row: With E, K2. (K4. K2tog) 4 times. With B, (K4. K2tog) 4 times. K2. 44 sts.
6th row: With B, P22. With E, P22.
7th row: With E, K2. (K3. K2tog) 4 times. With A, (K3. K2tog) 4 times. K2. 36 sts.
8th row: With A, P18. With E, P18.
9th row: With E, K2. (K2. K2tog) 4 times. With C, (K2. K2tog) 4 times. K2. 28 sts.
10th row: With C, P14. With E, P14.
11th row: With E, K2. (K1. K2tog) 4 times. With D, (K1. K2tog) 4 times. K2. 20 sts.
12th row: With D, P10. With E, P10.
13th row: With E, (K2tog) 5 times. With B, (K2tog) 5 times. 10 sts.
Break E leaving a long end. Draw E tightly through rem sts and fasten securely. With E, sew center back seam, changing to A to sew Lower Edging seam. •

PUZZLE POINTS BLANKET

Basic

MEASUREMENTS

Approx 50½"/128cm x 60"/152.5cm.

MATERIALS

YARN

Bernat® Blanket™ O'Go™, 10.5oz/300g O'Gos, each approx 220yd/201m (polyester) (6)

- 3 O'Gos in #42019 Rose Gold (A, B, C)
- 2 O'Gos in #42022 Art Nouveau (C, D, E)

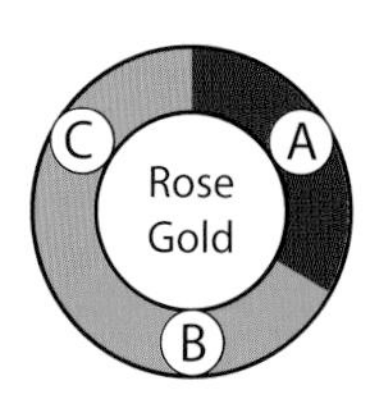

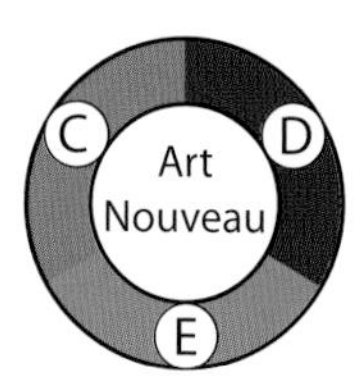

NEEDLES

- One size 11 (8mm) circular needle, 36"/91.5cm long, *or size needed to obtain gauge*

NOTIONS

- 2 stitch markers

GAUGE

7 sts and 14 rows = 4"/10cm in garter st.

TAKE TIME TO CHECK GAUGE.

NOTES

1) For this pattern, the colors in the O'Gos need to be separated (see page 2 for tips).

2) Work back and forth across circular needle in rows.

CHEVRON STRIP

Make 4 with C as Color 1, A as Color 2, and E as Color 3.

Make 2 with B as Color 1, D as Color 2, and E as Color 3.

BASE TRIANGLE

With Color 1, **cast on 3 sts.

1st row: (RS). Kfb. yo. PM. K1. PM. yo. Kfb. 7 sts.

2nd and alt rows: Knit, slipping markers.

3rd row: Kfb. K2. yo. Sm. K1. Sm. yo. K2. Kfb. 11 sts.

5th row: Kfb. Knit to marker. yo. Sm. K1. Sm. yo. Knit to last st. Kfb. 15 sts.

Cont as established, inc 4 sts every RS row to 39 sts on needle ending on a WS row. ** Do not break yarn.

CHEVRON SECTION

Next row: (RS). K1. ssk. Knit to marker. yo. Sm. K1. Sm yo. Knit to last 3 sts. K2tog. K1. 39 sts.

Next row: Knit.

Rep last 2 rows until Chevron Section at side edge measures 10"/25.5cm ,ending on a WS row. Break color 1.

With Color 2, cont as established until Chevron Section at side edge measures 16"/40.5cm, ending on a WS row. Break Color 2.

With Color 3, cont as established until Chevron Section at side edge measures 20"/51cm, ending on a WS row. Bind off.

SQUARE (MAKE 2)

With B, cast on 19 sts.

Work in garter st (knit every row) until work from beg measures 10"/25.5cm. Bind off.

TRIANGLE (MAKE 2)

With D, work from ** to ** as given for Base Triangle. Bind off.

FINISHING

Sew Chevron Strips, Triangles and Squares tog as seen in Assembly diagram, noting directional placement of each piece.

PUZZLE POINTS BLANKET

RIGHT BORDER

With RS facing and A, pick up and knit 98 sts up right edge of Blanket. Work in garter st (knit every row) for 2"/5cm ending on a RS row. Bind off.

LEFT BORDER

With RS facing and A, pick up and knit 98 sts down left edge of Blanket. Work as given for Right Border.

Assembly Diagram

E
Chevron Strip C A
Chevron Strip B D
Chevron Strip C A
E E E
A Triangle D
Square B
Square B
Triangle D A
E E E
A C Chevron Strip
D B Chevron Strip
A C Chevron Strip
D

TOP BORDER

With RS facing and E, pick up and knit 81 sts across top edge of Blanket. Work as given for Right Border.

BOTTOM BORDER

With RS facing and D, pick up and knit 81 sts across bottom edge of Blanket. Work as given for Right Border.

FRINGE

Cut strands of C 10"/25.5cm long. Fold each strand in half and knot into fringe through each st at top and bottom edge of Blanket. Trim fringe evenly. •

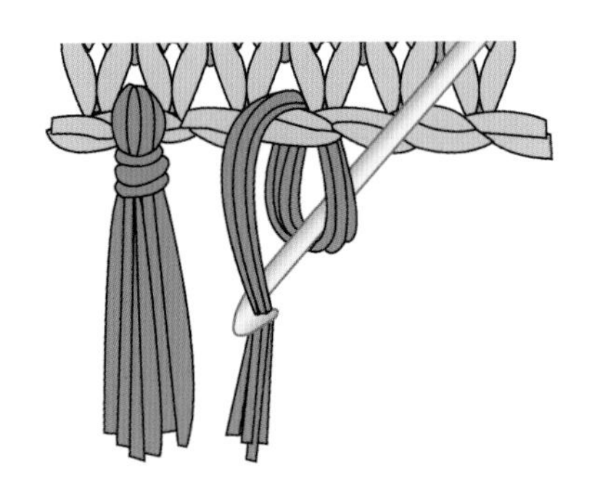

LET'S GO BEGINNER STRIPE SWEATER

Basic

SIZES

To fit bust measurement:

XS/S 28–34"/71–86.5cm

M 36–38"/91.5–96.5cm

L 40–42"/101.5–106.5cm

XL 44–46"/112–117cm

2/3XL 48–54"/122–137cm

4/5XL 56–62"/142–157.5cm

Finished bust:

XS/S 42"/106.5cm

M 46"/117cm

L 50"/127cm

XL 54"/137cm

2/3XL 58"/142cm

4/5XL 65"/165cm

MATERIALS

YARN

Caron® Colorama™ O'Go™, 6.4oz/180g O'Gos, each approx 228yd/208m (acrylic) (5)

- 5 (6, 7, 8, 9, 10) O'Gos in #68002 Tabby

NEEDLES

- One pair size 10 (6mm) knitting needles, *or size needed to obtain gauge*

NOTIONS

- 4 stitch markers
- Yarn needle

GAUGE

12 sts and 21 rows = 4"/10cm in Seed St.

TAKE TIME TO CHECK GAUGE.

NOTES

1) Cast on for Back and Front at same color change of O'Go to match striping as shown.

2) Sleeves are picked up from sides of Front and Back and worked down towards cuff.

3) Begin Sleeves at same color change of O'Go to match striping as shown.

4) The instructions are written for smallest size. If changes are necessary for larger size(s) the instructions will be written thus ( ). When only one number is given, it applies to all sizes.

BACK AND FRONT (MAKE ALIKE)

Cast on 63 (69-75-81-87-97) sts.

1st row: (RS). *K1. P1. Rep from * to last st. K1.

2nd row: *P1. K1. Rep from * to last st. P1.

Rep last 2 rows of (K1. P1) ribbing 5 times more, ending on a 2nd row (12 rows in total).

LET'S GO BEGINNER STRIPE SWEATER

Proceed in Seed St Pat as follows:

1st row: (RS). *P1. K1. Rep from * to last st. P1.

Rep last row for Seed St Pat until Back from beginning (beg) measures 24 (24-24½-24½-25-25)"/61 (61-62-62-63.5-63.5)cm, ending on a WS row.

Work 8 rows in (K1. P1) ribbing.

Cast off evenly in ribbing (take care to not cast off too tightly).

Place markers for shoulders 5½ (6-7-8-9-10½)"/12.5 (15-18-20.5-23-26.5)cm in from side edges - approx 10 (11-11-11-11-11)"/25.5 (28-28-28-28-28)cm left open for neck.

When Front and Back are complete, sew shoulder seams to markers.

Place markers for Sleeve pick up on side edges 8½ (9-9½-10-10-10½)"/21.5 (23-24.5-25.5-25.5-26.5)cm down from shoulder seams.

SLEEVES

With RS facing, pick up and knit 53 (55-59-61-61-65) sts evenly between markers on side edges of Front and Back.

Next row: (WS). *P1. K1. Rep from * to last st. P1.

Work in Seed St Pat for for a further 8 rows, ending on a WS row.

Keeping continuity of Seed St Pat, shape sides of Sleeves as follows:

Next row: (Dec row). K2tog. Pat to last 2 sts. K2tog.

Cont in Seed St Pat, AT SAME TIME, rep Dec row every following 10th row 6 times more. 39 (41-45-47-47-51) sts remain (rem).

Work even in Seed St Pat until Sleeve from beg (pick up row) measures 16½ (16½-16-15½-15½-15)"/42 (42-40.5-39.5-39.5-38)cm, ending on a RS row.

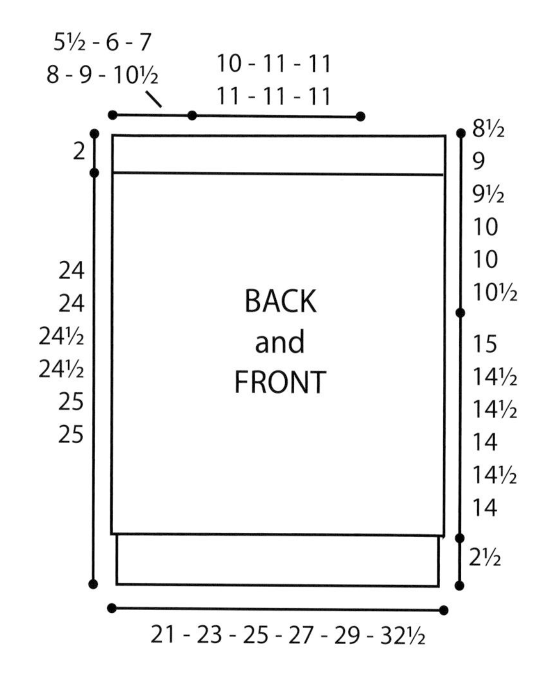

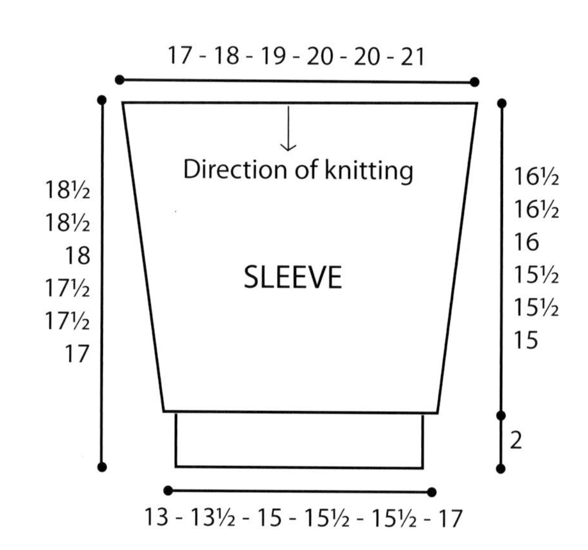

Next row: (WS-Dec row). P1. *K2tog. P1. Rep from * to last 2 (4-2-4-4-2) sts. (K1. P1) 1 (2-1-2-2-1) time(s). 27 (29-31-33-33-35) sts rem.

CUFF

Work 8 rows in (K1. P1) ribbing. Cast off in ribbing.

FINISHING

Sew side and sleeve seams. •

DOUBLE STRAND TEXTURED HAT

Easy

SIZE

One size to fit Adult.

MATERIALS

YARN

Caron® Big Donut™ O'Go™, 9.9oz/280g O'Gos, each approx 502yd/459m (acrylic) (4)

- 1 O'Go in #29011 Boston Cream or #29007 Blue Velvet

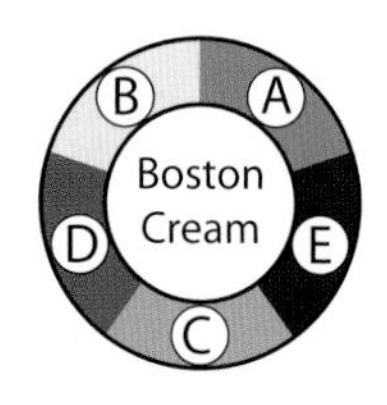

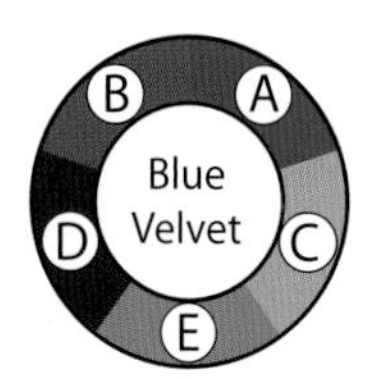

NEEDLES

- One pair size 10 (6mm) knitting needles, *or size needed to obtain gauge*

NOTION

- Yarn needle

GAUGE

10 sts and 22 rows = 4"/10cm with 2 strands of yarn held tog in Beehive Pat.

TAKE TIME TO CHECK GAUGE.

NOTE

For this pattern, the colors in the O'Go need to be separated (see page 2 for tips).

HAT

With 1 strand each of A and B held tog, cast on 63 sts.

1st row: (RS). K2. *P1. K1. Rep from * to last st. K1.

2nd row: *K1. P1. Rep from * to last st. K1.

Rep last 2 rows of (K1. P1) ribbing for 4"/10cm, ending on a RS row. Break A and B.

Next row (dec row): With 1 strand each of C and D held tog, P6. *P2tog. P5. Rep from * to last st. P1. 55 sts.

BEEHIVE PAT

1st row: (RS). K1. *K1below. K1. Rep from * to end of row.

2nd row: Knit.

3rd row: K2. *K1below. K1. Rep from * to last st. K1.

4th row: Knit.

Rep these 4 rows for Beehive Pat until Hat measures approx 10"/25.5cm from beg, ending on a 4th row of pat.

SHAPE TOP

1st row: (RS). K1. *K1below. K3tog. K1below. K1. Rep from * end of row. 37 sts rem.

2nd row: Knit.

3rd row: K2. *K1below. K3tog. Rep from * to last 3 sts. K1below. K2. 21 sts rem.

4th row: Knit.

5th row: K1. *K1below. K3tog. Rep from * to end of row. 11 sts rem. Break yarn leaving a long end. Draw end tightly through rem sts and fasten securely.

FINISHING

Sew center back seam, reversing seam for cuff turnback.

POMPOM

Wind E around 4 fingers 100 times. Remove from fingers. Tie tightly in the middle with long strand of yarn (this will be used to attach pompom to Hat). Cut loops at both ends and trim to smooth round shape. Attach securely to top of Hat. •

HEARTWARMING SCARF

Basic

MEASUREMENTS

Narrow: 4"/10cm x 55"/140cm.
Wide: 8"/20.5cm x 80"/203cm.

MATERIALS

YARN

Red Heart® Super Saver™ O'Go™, 5oz/141g O'Gos, each approx 236yd/215m (acrylic) (4)

Version 1:

- 1 (2) O'Go in #7195 Jeweltone

Version 2:

- 1 (2) O'Go in #7136 Forest

NEEDLES

- One pair size 9 (5.5mm) knitting needles, *or size needed to obtain gauge*

NOTION

- Yarn needle

GAUGE

16 sts and 22 rows = 4"/10cm in St st.
TAKE TIME TO CHECK GAUGE.

NOTE

The instructions are written for smaller size. If changes are necessary for larger size the instructions will be written thus ( ). When only one number is given, it applies to both sizes.

SCARF

Cast on 16 (32) sts.
1st and 2nd row: *K2. P2. Rep from * to end of row.
3rd and 4th rows: Knit.
Rep last 4 rows until Scarf measures 55 (80)"/140 (203)cm from beg, ending on a 1st row.
Bind off. •

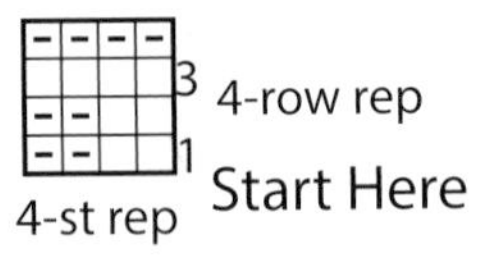

Stitch Key

☐ = Knit on RS rows. Purl on WS rows.
⊟ = Purl on RS rows. Knit on WS rows.